LIMITS OF PAPAL AUTHORITY OVER THE LITURGY

by

Father Chad Ripperger, PhD

Sensus Traditionis Press
Keenesburg, CO 80643

In Honorem Matris Pulchrae Dilectionis

Table of Contents

Acknowledgments

There are many people who should receive some form of credit for helping this author bring this text to fruition. Unfortunately, not all of them can be mentioned, but a few need to be selected out as providing returned suggestions that helped in key ways. I would like to thank Fr. Cliff Ermatinger for content and suggestions. Dr. Mike Sirilla, who took time out of his busy schedule, to review the book for logical consistency and to ensure conclusions were not overstated. Likewise, Fr. Josh Stengel who also provided suggestions and input to make sure the conclusions were moderated. I also thank Lisa Fischer, Fawaz Yasi, Fr. Dan McElheron and Leo Severino for helping the readability of the text. Susan Follansbee is to be credited for helping the readability by doing a manuscript edit. I would also like to thank Dr. Peter Kwasniewski and Ryan Grant for providing key citations and to Ryan Grant, again, for providing a historical review as well as a key distinction in regards to Scripture.

Introduction

In recent years, there has been a renewed discussion about the nature of papal authority over the liturgy. With the advent of *Traditiones Custodes* and the subsequent documents, there is renewed interest in the question of whether a pope can suppress a rite, and if so, under what conditions. This also brings to the fore the discussion of what authority, if any, does the pope have over the liturgy. This is not just a question of today, but it has been a question that has occurred historically within the Church. When one peruses the various writers on the subject, there tends to be two extremes, *viz.*, those who say he does not have authority to make liturgical changes, or restrict them severely to such a point as rendering it such that he has no authority, practically speaking, and those who think the pope can do whatever he pleases in relation to the rites, including the rite of the Holy Sacrifice of the Mass.

As one reads the various modern authors, there appears to be a particular phenomenon occurring in the discussion. Most authors cite very few sources in the tradition to support their conclusions. Of those who do cite various sources, very few are from the tradition and the sources tend to be cited in isolation without a full theological context as is seen in this discussion in the tradition of the Church. A few authors are doing the research and do cite various aspects of the tradition, so progress is being made slowly.

The goal of this book is not to settle the question in all of its facets. Such an endeavor would require a much more extensive work. The goal of this book is to bring the discussion into focus by basing the conclusions on solid Catholic principle derived from the official teaching of the Church, the popes, the saints, and theologians throughout the history of the Church. One of the hallmarks of a protracted discussion on any topic is a lack of isolation and identifying the principles, which serve as the premises in the discussion. It is not until the premises are properly identified that a discussion can even be had about those premises, since ultimately the disagreement over conclusions is not rooted in the conclusion itself, but either in the truth of the premises or the reasoning process itself. For that reason, it is the goal of the book to begin the process of identifying the principles and teachings of the Church, so as to reach conclusions through sound reasoning. It is not the intention of this author to attack any rite, form of the Mass, the various members of the Church who offer specific rites, etc. Such an *ad hominem* approach will serve no purpose, but to erode charity. May God bless the reader of this book and may Our Lady grant him the grace to recognize any possible truth contained in it.

Chapter I: Nature of Authority

In a discussion about papal authority over the liturgy, one would not think it would be necessary to discuss the nature of authority in context of theological debate where everyone should already have such a basic and essential knowledge. However, one can quickly see that in the discussions by various authors in the area of papal authority over the liturgy, numerous distinctions that should be being made are not, and it leads to confusion and conclusions which are either excessive in their assertions or fall short of the reality of the papal authority over the liturgy or its limitations. For that reason, a chapter must be dedicated to the nature of authority so that both its binding force when legitimate as well as its restrictions are properly known.

I. The Nature of Authority Itself[1]

It is sometimes said that 90 percent of philosophy is an argument over the definition of terms. Since a definition is the "formulation of the essence of the thing," a few definitions have to be parsed out so that their theological application in the area of papal authority over the liturgy can be properly understood. Any student of theology knows that many of the terms in theology are adopted from philosophy and so one's philosophical understanding of certain areas of knowledge determines one's theology. This is no more evident than in metaphysics but, in this particular case, the focus is actually in the area of definitions that pertain to ethics, specifically justice, which deals with rights in relation to authority. Therefore, it is necessary to observe the definitions of power, right, and authority.

Power among philosophers and theologians is called *active potency* which is defined as: "the principle of change or of acting upon

---

[1]This section of the chapter comes in substance from Ripperger, *The Nature and Psychology of Diabolic Influence*, chpt. 4. It is also found in his book *Dominion*.

another inasmuch as that is in the other thing; the principle of efficient action on another; ability to make."[2] The actual term "power" has essentially the same definition: "**1.** In general, ability to do or make; capacity for acting. **2.** A principle of acting upon something else; an active potency."[3] In effect, a power is the ability to bring about change in some other thing.

Historically, the Church always made the distinction between the power of orders and the power of jurisdiction. In regard to jurisdiction, in the old *Catholic Encyclopedia* the following entry is found:

> The Church founded by Christ for the salvation of men needs, like every society, a regulating power (the authority of the Church). This power Christ has bestowed upon it. Directly before His Ascension He gave to the Apostles collectively the commission, and with it the authority, to proclaim His doctrine to all nations, to baptize them, and to teach them to observe all things that He had commanded (Matt., xxviii, 18 sqq.). It may be noted here that the Decree "Lamentabili sane", of 3 July, 1907, rejects (n. 52 sqq.) the doctrine that Christ did not desire to found a permanent, unchangeable Church endowed with authority. It is customary to speak of a threefold office of the Church: the office of teaching (prophetic office), the priestly office, and the pastoral office (governing office), also, therefore, of the threefold authority of the Church, that is, the *teaching* authority, *ministerial* authority, and *ruling* authority. Since, however, the teaching of the Church is authoritative, the teaching authority is traditionally included in the ruling authority; regularly, therefore, only the ministerial authority and the ruling authority are distinguished. By ministerial

[2]Wuellner, *Dictionary of Scholastic Philosophy*, p. 236.

[3]Ibid.

> authority, which is conferred by an act of consecration, is meant the inward, and, because of its indelible character, permanent capacity to perform acts by which Divine grace is transmitted. By ruling authority, which is conferred by the Church (*missio canonica*, canonical mission), is understood the authority to guide and rule the Church of God. Jurisdiction, in so far as it covers the relations of man to God, is called *jurisdiction of the internal forum* or jurisdiction of the forum of Heaven (*jurisdictio poli*).[4]

We see a distinction between the ministerial authority, which is sometimes called the power of orders, and the ruling authority, which is called the power of jurisdiction. This distinction of powers is important because it gets to the real issue of authority in relationship to the authority the pope has over the liturgy, as will be seen.

In regard to the power of orders, Ludwig Ott has the following entry:

> The Power of Order
> The Sacrament of Order confers a permanent spiritual power on the recipient. (*De fide.*) Cf. D 960 et seq. In the sacramental character are rooted those spiritual powers which are transferred to the ordinand in the individual grades of Order. They are directed pre-eminently to the Holy Eucharist. The Deacon receives the power of immediately serving the bishop and the priest at the offering of the Eucharistic sacrifice and of dispensing Holy Communion. The priest principally receives the power of consecration and of absolution (D 961), the bishop the power of ordination.[5]

---

[4]See OCE under jurisdiction.

[5]Ott, *Fundamentals of Catholic Dogma*, p. 457.

It has been a constant tradition of the Church that a priest at the time of his ordination receives a power by which he is able to command the sacraments to occur, namely, to consecrate the Eucharist, to absolve sins, etc. Yet, as was seen in the quote above from the old *Catholic Encyclopedia*, there was also another power called jurisdiction, and jurisdiction determines the actual use of the priestly power.

Wuellner, whose philosophical dictionary is considered somewhat of a standard in the Thomistic/Scholastic/Catholic philosophical community, defines authority as follows: "the moral power to command or enforce obedience in the community. Moral authority, a right granted by moral law to impose obligation on the acts of others; moral power to bind persons to act and not to act in certain ways under penalty of sinning."[6] In this definition we see several things of note. The first is that authority is a moral power and by "moral" power we mean that which pertains to reason.[7]

What this means is that something moral is that which is perceived by reason and no other human faculty. Due to the fact that the third category of natural inclination of the natural law in intelligent creatures includes a natural inclination to obey God,[8] we know that it pertains to the actual intelligence or reason of the creature to be able to perceive or to know that the individual who has authority has the right to bind another. In other words, God built into human beings a natural inclination which inclines the intellect to recognize (know) the binding force (obligation) to execute the command of the one who has legitimate authority over them. Therefore, authority on the side of the one receiving the command is the structure built into the mind to

---

[6]Wuellner, *Dictionary of Scholastic Philosophy*, p. 26.

[7]See De Malo, q. 2, a. 4. For further discussion of the term "moral" and how it is used in the morality of St. Thomas, see Ripperger, *The Morality of the Exterior Act*, chpt. 4.

[8]See II Sent., d. 39, q. 3, a. 2.

perceive the binding force of the command. On the side of the one who has authority, it is a right granted by the natural law (we shall see later also the Divine Positive Law) by which one can command another to do something. Therefore, in relationship to the first thing to be noted in the definition above, it is to be recognized that authority pertains to reason or intellect of the creature who receives the command.[9]

The second that should be noted from above has to do with the word *command* in the definition. Command is defined as: "**1**. Having or exercising authority, jurisdiction, or control. **2**. Issuing an order; directing. An act of the reason of the superior or lawgiver requiring subjects to take definite action to an end."[10] Command can sometimes simply mean the exercising of authority. However, normally a command is the issuing of an order which requires the individual to do something or to stop doing something.

The third thing of importance in the above definition has to do with the term "right." In the modern political context, the term "right" is subject to all sorts of misunderstandings. However philosophically, the definition of a right is clear:

---

[9]Nevins in *The Maryknoll Catholic Dictionary* (p. 61) defines authority as: "a person in command or who has jurisdiction." On page 62, he has the following entry: "Authority, Ecclesiastical: because the Church is a perfect society, having within itself the means for the sanctification of its members and of giving order to God, the Church has authority in spiritual matters and in those temporal matters which affect the spiritual. The authority of the Church is the authority of Jesus Christ who delegated His authority to St. Peter and through him to the popes and bishops." The *Oxford English Dictionary* (p. 572) under authority has: "1. Power or right to enforce obedience; moral or legal supremacy; the right to command, or give ultimate decision. ... In possession of power over others." Under the entry for command (p. 688) it has: "To order, enjoin, bid with authority influence. Power of control, disposal, or direction; mastery; possession with full power to use; under one's control."

[10]Wuellner, *Dictionary of Scholastic Philosophy*, p. 52.

> A right is properly said to be defined in general [as]: *that which some owe to others as theirs.* Hence, it expresses a twofold relation, objective and moral, as will be clear immediately. **That which some owe**, designates a threefold material object of right, which are either a *thing* or an *action* to be exercised freely by the subject of the right or due *renderings* or *omissions* of others. ...**That some owe to others**, expresses in moral relation, which consists in a rendering to the person to which something is owed, referring to all others.[11]

In this definition of right there are a few things that are of importance. The first is that a right involves a moral claim, namely, others by their reason or intellectual grasp are bound to render to an individual something to which he has a right. Second, all rights bind others to render some kind of action or thing in relationship to the one to whom it is owed.[12] As the individual with authority who commands him, the

---

[11]Ballerini, *Compendium Theologiae Moralis*, vol. 1, p. 906: "Ius proprie dictum in genere definiri potest: *id quod alicui ab aliis debetur tanquam suum.* Unde duplicem relationem exprimit, obiectivam et moralem, ut statim patebit. **Quod debetur**, designat triplex obiectum iuris materiale, quod sunt sive *res*, sive *actio* a subiecto iuris libere exercenda, sive aliorum *praestationes* vel *omissiones* debitae. ...**Ab aliis alicui debetur**, exprimit relationem *moralem*, qua consistit in praelatione personae cui aliquid ut suum debitur, relate ad alias omnes. Sic ius apparet in possidente tanquam *facultas moralis inviolabilis personae aliquid faciendi, habendi, exigendi in proprium exclusive commodum.*" Nevins, *The Maryknoll Catholic Dictionary*, p. 494: "Right: A moral power by which a person may claim something is due to him or as belonging to him." See also Ballerini, *Compendium Theologiae Moralis*, vol. 1, p. 364: "Nomine iuris, presse sumpti, et quod ad praesens attinet, intelligitur vel id, quod alteri debitur, *iustumque* dici solet aut *equale*, et sic est obiectum, quod iustitia intendit, quodque ipsa cuique tribuit."

[12]See op. cit., p. 907: "**Ius unius necessario infert** *aliorum obligationem correlativam.*" See also, Wuellner, *Dictionary of Scholastic Philosophy*, p. 269:

one who is commanded must submit in his will.[13] Therefore, the one in authority has the the right to command and to be obeyed.

Wuellner includes in his entry under right the following: "**Natural right**, right coming to man from the Author of nature and directing from the natural law fulfillment of duties of this law."[14] This observes two things: (1) that the possessor of a natural right receives that right coming from God and, therefore, others do not have a right to set that natural right aside except insofar as: (2) that all rights in relationship to creatures are circumscribed by their natural law. In other words, all rights pertaining to human beings are conditional rights and the conditions that determine those rights constitute the natural law itself. By extension we can say that since God is the author of the natural law, all human rights and their limits are ultimately determined by God. This is important in relationship to papal authority, as even his authority is not unlimited or absolute, for only God has absolute rights, but papal authority is circumscribed by the Natural Law and by the Divine Positive Law, as will be discussed throughout this text. Our rights are ultimately conceded to us by God. Therefore, an individual, who has a right over something or someone, has a moral claim in relation to the disposition of the thing or person, and others have an obligation to allow or observe the individual's determination of the dispositions. For example, if one owns a statue, that owner has a moral claim as to the disposition of the statue, *viz.*, what is to be done with the statue. His right of disposition is only circumscribed by the limitations of the Natural Law or Divine Positive

---

"Right: *subjective right.* The inviolable power to do, hold, or claim something as one's own."

[13]This is why Edwards in the *Encyclopedia of Philosophy,* p. 216 observes: "Authority in a *de facto* sense exists whenever a man *recognizes* another is *entitled* to command him."

[14]Wuellner, *Dictionary of Scholastic Philosophy*, p. 270.

Law.

Edwards in the *Encyclopedia of Philosophy* under the entry on authority has:

> "authority" is often defined as "legitimate power." Nevertheless, many writers insist, with de Jouvenel, that "power is something very distinct from authority. The distinguishing mark of the latter is that it is exercised only over those who voluntarily accept it."[15]

This observation by Edwards provides an important distinction between authority and power. It was seen above that power is "the ability to effect change" but that is different from having the *right* to command those changes to be done or made. Here, Edwards is noting that if the people in a particular society do not accept someone who is in a position of power, it is not said that he has legitimate authority. In other words, it is possible for someone in a government to obtain the power to enforce his commands, but that does not give him the right to do so. This is known by the common experience of man. For example, if an individual encounters a misbehaving child in a supermarket and he is not the parent of the child, he has the physical power to take the child and spank the child. That does not give him the right to spank him. What gives him the right to spank him is the authority over the child, (*i.e.*, the moral claim in relationship to the disposition of the child). Common human experience is replete with examples: the Nazis had the power to exterminate the Jews; it did not give them the right to do so, etc.[16]

So, to give a fuller understanding to the nature of authority, we may define it as: "a right (moral claim) of disposition, either in

---

[15]Vol. 1, p. 215.

[16]This distinction holds true even in relation to the papacy as the subsequent chapters will address.

action or thing, on the side of the one with the authority in relation to others by which they must follow his legitimate commands." This binds those who are under the authority in those matters over which he has right of disposition or right of command. One may have the right to command, (*i.e.*, the authority) and yet not the power to enforce the command which, again, indicates that power and authority are distinct.

II. Natural Law and Divine Positive Law

When considering the difference between the Natural Law and the Divine Positive Law, we recognize that both are divine laws insofar as they proceed from God and both are binding. However, when one looks at the definition of divine law, one discovers that there are differences between the two:

> **Law, Divine.** I. Eternal: "the Divine Reason or Will of God, commanding the observance and forbidding the disturbance of the natural order of things" (St. Augustine); called "the natural law" when perceived through the light of reason. Total ignorance (q.v.) of its primary precepts (*e.g.*, "evil must be avoided") or continued ignorance of the secondary precepts (*e.g.*, "thou shalt not steal") is impossible.
> II. Positive: precepts known through Revelation. These fall into three classes: (*a*) moral – a more explicit determination of the natural law; (*b*) ceremonial – with respect to the Sacraments and the Mass; (c) juridical – with respect to the constitution authority of the Church.[17]

Divine Positive Laws are the precepts which are known through Revelation and these would include things such as the precepts of

[17]Attwater, *A Catholic Dictionary*, p. 302.

charity,[18] Christ commanding the Apostles to offer Mass in commemoration of Him,[19] etc. However, as the definition points out, it also deals with the authority given to the Church, and this pertains to those matters now under consideration, *viz.*, the right of the pope over the liturgy.

III. Authority *ad Personam* and Authority *ad Rem* or Who Has What Authority

When asked who has authority over whom, the question may be answered in a general sort of way by simply saying: whoever has the power to command the individual either according to the Natural Law or the Divine Positive Law. However, it is important to parse out specifically who has the authority according to both the Divine Positive Law and the Natural Law. Such authority often comes in the form of an office.

The *Oxford English Dictionary* defines office as: "**1.** to perform divine service: officiate; **2.** to perform in the way of duty or service." This gives an initial sense of what the term *office* actually means. Another definition would be: "(1) any obligatory service, duty, obligation...(2) an official duty, service, employment, business."[20] St. Thomas makes an important observation regarding the matter: "office is said by comparison to action; however grade is said according to order of superiority and inferiority; but to state, immobility is required in that which pertains to the condition of the person."[21] St. Thomas is essentially saying that an office has something to do with action, *i.e.*,

---

[18]Mark 12:30.

[19]Luke 22:19.

[20]Deferrari, *A Lexicon of Saint Thomas Aquinas*, p. 766.

[21]ST II-II, q. 183, a. 1, ad 3: "Officium dicitur per comparationem ad actum; gradus autem dicitur secundum ordinem superioritatis et inferioritatis; sed ad statum requiritur immobilitas in eo quod pertinet ad conditionem personae."

action which is obligatory. Grade is said simply in relationship to whether one thing is above it or not. But state requires an immobility pertaining to the condition of the person. It is possible, however, that a person can enter into a different state, which is also the reception of an office, insofar as the state is the condition of the individual; for example, a man may enter into a different state insofar as he now becomes a father, but fatherhood is also an office which requires certain actions in relationship to his child.

From this we can extrapolate a full definition of office. An office may be defined as "a condition or quality of an individual to perform an obligatory duty or service in relation to others." Contained in this definition are two things: the first is that an office is a quality or condition of the individual and by this is understood that there is something in the individual, which reason recognizes that places him in a specific relationship to others in a particular manner; for example, the person who has the office of fatherhood is in a specific condition or has a specific quality in relationship to his children, that is, he is the origin of their material existence insofar as he provided matter from which they sprang. The second is a relationship, or we may even say condition, that obligates him to specific kinds of action in relationship to other people (*ad personam*). That obligation or duty requires that the individual render to others or act in relationship to others in specific ways (*ad rem*). Since all duties imply rights, due to the fact that someone who has a duty is bound to perform the action that pertains to that duty, therefore, since he is bound, he has a right to fulfill his duty. This means that others must observe his right to fulfill his duty; for example, the various members of the state have an obligation to observe the right of the father to fulfill his duties in relationship to his children (*i.e.*, he has a right to properly raise them). The term "ad rem" refers to either (a) the thing over which a person has authority or (b) something specific in relation to the thing, if the authority is restricted or determined in a specific way to the thing. This right which arises from an office grants one authority, per the definition of authority above, in relation to the person or things he is bound in duty to act. Therefore, three criteria for an office are: (1) it is a relationship (2) established by the Natural Law or Divine Positive Law (3) in which service of another or others is obligatory.

This is important, since the papacy is an office which is given by God to certain individuals throughout time. As an office, the pope has authority, but that authority is circumscribed, as we saw above, by the Divine Positive Law, which grants him the authority of his office and the Natural Law, since the Divine Positive Law also commands us to obey the Natural Law.[22] The papacy, when considered as an office, constitutes a relation a particular man has to the whole Church and to Christ as His vicar or servant. It is an office established by the Divine Positive Law, and since the Divine Positive Law commands obedience to the Natural Law, the authority of the papacy is circumscribed by the Divine Positive Law and Natural Law. So the pope has authority of certain matters (*ad rem*) in certain ways (also *ad rem*) in relation to others (*ad personam*) and these are determined by the Divine Positive Law and the Natural Law. Essentially, this means his authority is not unlimited or absolute, even though it is supreme, but is finite. By supreme is understood that there is no authority greater than the pope or above the pope on earth,[23] but since all authority comes from God,[24] God Himself has set the limitations of that authority via the Divine Positive Law and Natural Law.

---

[22]This is why Christ said in Matthew 19:17: "keep the commandments." Here the reference is to the Ten Commandments, which are an explication of the natural law inclinations placed in man.

[23]See next chapter.

[24]Romans 13:1.

Chapter II: The Pope's Authority over the Liturgy

Since Christ entrusted the elements of sanctification to the Apostles and their successors, the proper guardians of the sacraments and rituals are the members of the Magisterium. Pope Pius XII discusses the authority of the Magisterium over the liturgy in *Mediator Dei* in several places.

> Since, therefore, it is the priest chiefly who performs the sacred liturgy in the name of the Church, its organization, regulation and form cannot but be dependent upon Church authority. This conclusion, based on the nature of Christian worship itself, is further confirmed by the testimony of history.[1]

Even during and after the Second Vatican Council, the documents coming out of the Vatican repeatedly stated that no priest can change the liturgy on his own authority.[2] But two things are of importance in the above statement by Pius XII. The first is that since the performing of the liturgy is an act of the priest as a public person, he acts as an agent and servant of the Church, and therefore, does so in the name of the Church, which means his offering of the rites of the Church is subject to the regulation by those who have authority over the liturgy in the Church. The second is that this reality is testified by history. It simply is not possible to reference all of these instances where the Church has made this observation, but suffice it to say, the reality of this authority over the liturgy will become clear from the various

---

[1]Pius, XII, *Mediator Dei*, para. 44: "Quoniam igitur sacra Liturgia imprimis a sacerdotibus Ecclesiae nomine absolvitur, idcirco eius ordinatio, moderatio ac forma ab Ecclesiae auctoritate non pendere non potest. Quod quidem sicut ex ipsa christiani cultus natura consequitur, ita etiam historiae documentis confirmatur."

[2]Among others see *Sacrosanctum Concilium*, para. 22.

statements throughout this text.

Pope Pius XII continues:

> Additional proof of this indefeasible right of the ecclesiastical hierarchy lies in the circumstances that the sacred liturgy is intimately bound up with doctrinal propositions which the Church proposes to be perfectly true and certain, and must as a consequence conform to the decrees respecting Catholic faith issued by the supreme teaching authority of the Church with a view to safeguarding the integrity of the religion revealed by God.[3]

In addition to the conferring of rights by Christ to the Apostles and their successors over the elements of sanctification, the right to regulate the liturgy is a necessary consequence of the connection the liturgy has to doctrinal propositions. This will become very important in the discussion of the limits of papal authority, however, the main thing to recognize is that, since it is the duty of the pope to "confirm the brethren,"[4] then he must be able to regulate the liturgy in order to protect the doctrinal integrity of the Church. As will be seen later, the tendency of heretics is to change the liturgy and so it is necessary to be able to protect the Church from heresy by regulating the liturgy, so that nothing heretical is introduced into it.

Pope Pius XII then goes on to make an important distinction in regard to the liturgy:

---

[3]Pius, XII, *Mediator Dei*, para. 45: "Aliud praeterea est, quod inconcussum hoc Ecclesiasticae Hierarchiae ius comprobat, quod nimirum sacra Liturgia cum iis doctrinae principiis arctissime coniungitur, quae ab Ecclesia ut certissimae veritatis capita proponuntur, atque adeo catholicae fidei praeceptis conformanda est, quae supremi Magisterii auctoritas edidit ad divinitus patefactae religionis integritatem tutandam."

[4]Luke 22:32.

> The sacred liturgy, consequently, does not decide or determine independently and of itself what is of Catholic faith. More properly, since the liturgy is also a profession of eternal truths, and subject, as such, to the supreme teaching authority of the Church, it can supply proofs and testimony, quite clearly, of no little value, towards the determination of a particular point of Christian doctrine. But if one desires to differentiate and describe the relationship between faith and the sacred liturgy in absolute and general terms, it is perfectly correct to say, "Lex credendi legem statuat supplicandi"—let the rule of belief determine the rule of prayer.[5]

This statement provides several things of importance. The first is that the liturgy is not a theological source[6] except in conjunction with other theological sources, such as Revelation, judgments of the Magisterium or tradition, etc. While the liturgical texts as monuments of tradition do provide proof and testimony to the doctrine of the faith, it cannot be the only source. This will become more important in relation to the length of that testimony in the liturgy. If something can be demonstrated to be in the liturgy *ab initio* or from the very beginning of Church history, such as the times of the Apostles, then

---

[5]Pius, XII, *Mediator Dei*, para. 48: "Atque eodem fere modo Ecclesia ac Ss. Patres, cum de aliqua veritate dubia controversaque disceptabatur, a venerandis etiam ritibus ex antiquitate traditis lumen petere non praeteriere. Itaque notum et venerandum illud habetur effatum: «Legem credendi lex statuat supplicandi» 45 . Sacra igitur Liturgia catholicam fidem absolute suaque vi non designat neque constituit; sed potius, cum sit etiam veritatum caelestium, professio, quae Supremo Ecclesiae Magisterio subicitur, argumenta ac testimonia suppeditare potest, non parvi quidem momenti, ad peculiare decernendum christianae doctrinae caput. Quodsi volumus eas, quae inter fidem sacramque Liturgiam intercedunt, rationes absoluto generalique modo internoscere ac determinare, iure meritoque dici potest: 'Lex credendi legem statuat supplicandi.'."

[6]Here that term is used in the formal theological sense.

it will have a much greater theological weight, or more technically, its theological note will be higher than if it is something that is novel or more recent.

The second thing of importance in the above quote is that again, the liturgy is subject to the supreme authority of the Church; more overtly stated, it will be subject to papal authority, as will be seen shortly. The third thing of importance is the sequence of the phrase that has been long in the tradition of *lex credendi legem statuat supplicandi*. This is sometimes contracted to *lex credendi, lex orandi*. Pius XII is essentially observing that it is what the Church proposes for belief that determines how it prays. Again this will become important in the discussions of limitation of authority over the liturgy.

Yet, there is a proper sequence that the pope is observing. It is not the case that what we pray determines what we believe in a *doctrinal* sense, even though it is a theological source, since it has to be verified or supported by other theological sources. The reason is precisely that heretics change the liturgy to conform to their heresy. Rather, it is what we believe that determines how we pray. This is why one must understand when the phrase is reversed into *lex orandi, lex credendi*, it has to be understood in a very specific way. That the law of belief determines the law of prayer is the order of dependence of one on the other, *i.e.*, the formal content of the prayer of the Church is determined by the doctrine of the Church. However, *psychologically,* the belief system of the people is often determined by the formal content of the Church's prayer. The liturgy is a teacher and so what people see on Sundays when they go to Mass constitutes an intellectual formation about the sacred mysteries. This is why *how* a priest offers Mass is of prime importance, since it will often teach people what the Church actually believes regarding the doctrines of the Church. This is to be understood in a twofold way. The first is that the formal content of the prayers at Mass or other liturgical and para-liturgical actions of the Church teach people what the Church believes about specific doctrines. But secondly, it also tells people the various weights with which these things are to be held. For example, the

Church teaches that the Eucharist is the Body, Blood, Soul and Divinity of Jesus Christ, and as such is God, and therefore, is due the highest form of worship; if it is handled like common bread, people will either not believe it is God or they will believe that is how God is to be handled, approached, and treated, *i.e.*, it will diminish their Fear of the Lord.

The last passage from Pius XII that needs to be considered begins to lay the groundwork for a series of distinctions in the subsequent chapters that are of prime importance.

> It follows from this that the Sovereign Pontiff alone enjoys the right to recognize and establish any practice touching the worship of God, to introduce and approve new rites, as also to modify those he judges to require modification.[7]

This passage essentially reaffirms the teaching of the Church throughout time that the ultimate authority over the liturgy belongs to the pope.[8] Since the pope has the plenitude of power in matters of discipline,[9] this follows from his supreme jurisdiction.[10]

---

[7]Pius, XII, *Mediator Dei*, para. 58: "Quamobrem uni Summo Pontifici ius est quemlibet de divino cultu agendo morem recognoscere ac statuere, novos inducere ac probare ritus, eosque etiam immutare, quos quidem immutandos iudicaverit."

[8]See Oppenheim, *Institutiones Systematico-Historicae in Sacram Liturgiam*, p. 53-55.

[9]Denz. 1827. See also Ott, *Fundamentals of Catholic Dogma*, p. 285: "The Pope possesses full and supreme power of jurisdiction over the whole Church, not merely in matters of faith and morals, but also in Church discipline and in the government of the Church. (*De Fide*.)"

[10]Denz. 1831. That regulation of the liturgy by the pope pertains to jurisdiction will be seen in a subsequent chapter. Ott, *Fundamentals of Catholic Dogma*, p. 285: "Supreme power in the Church, that is, there is no jurisdiction

The last text to observe is that of the Council of Trent, which is quoted here at length:

> It declares furthermore, that in the dispensation of the sacraments, the Church may, according to circumstances, times and places, determine or change whatever she may judge most expedient for the benefit of those receiving them or for the veneration of the sacraments; and this power has always been hers. The Apostle seems to have clearly intimated this when he said: Let a man so account of us as of the ministers of Christ, and the dispensers of the mysteries of God; and that he himself exercised this power, as in many other things so in this sacrament, is sufficiently manifest, for after having given some instructions regarding its use, he says: "The rest I will set in order when I come." Wherefore, though from the beginning of the Christian religion the use of both forms has not been infrequent, yet since that custom has been already very widely changed, holy mother Church, cognizant of her authority in the administration of the sacraments, has, induced by just and weighty reasons, approved this custom of

---

possessing a greater or equally great power. The power of the Pope transcends both the power of each individual bishop and also of all the other bishops together. The bishops collectively (apart from the Pope), therefore, are not equal to or superior to the Pope. ...A full power, that is, the Pope possesses of himself alone, the whole fullness of the Church power of jurisdiction and not merely a greater share than the other bishops taken individually or conjointly. Thus the Pope can rule independently on any matter, which comes under the sphere of the Church's jurisdiction without the concurrence of the other bishops or of the rest of the Church." Ibid, p. 286: "As the supreme lawgiver of the Church, the Pope is not legally bound by ecclesiastical decisions and usages, but by divine law alone. This demands that the papal power, in consonance with its purpose, should be employed for the building-up of the Mystical Body of Christ, not for its destruction (2 Cor. 10:8. The divine law, therefore, is an efficacious brake on arbitrariness. The third Gallican article, which demanded a far-reaching limitation of the exercise of the Papal power, was properly rejected. D 1324)."

> communicating under either species and has decreed that it be considered the law, which may not be repudiated or changed at pleasure without the authority of the Church.[11]

This passage needs careful unpacking, so much so, in fact, that it will be addressed again under a different aspect in a subsequent chapter. However, first note that the Council of Trent is making it very clear that the Church has the authority over the liturgy. This is contrary to those who argue that the Church, Magisterium, or pope does not have the authority to make changes to the liturgy. Based upon the observations above, this indicates that the pope has a right, *i.e.*, the authority to make changes to the liturgy.

This passage from Trent is also cited subsequently by numerous doctors, theologians, and authors as indicating the power of the papacy over the liturgy, save the substance of the sacraments. This gives us our first indication that there are limitations of the authority of the pope over the liturgy. As will be seen again at greater length, he does not have the authority to change the substance of the sacraments, *e.g.*, he could not change the matter of the Eucharist to

---

[11]Council of Trent, Session 21, c. 2: "Praeterea declarat hanc potestatem perpetuo in Ecclesia fuisse ut in sacramentorum dispensatione salva illorum substantia ea statueret vel mutaret quae suscipientium utilitati seu ipsorum sacramentorum venerationi pro rerum temporum et locorum varietate magis expedire iudicaret. Id autem apostolus non obscure visus est innuisse cum ait: sic nos existimet homo ut ministros Christi et dispensatores mysteriorum Dei; atque ipsum quidem hac potestate usum esse satis constat cum in multis aliis tum in hoc ipso sacramento cum ordinatis nonnullis circa eius usum: cetera inquit cum venero disponam. Quare agnoscens sancta mater Ecclesia hanc suam in administratione sacramentorum auctoritatem licet ab initio christianae religionis non infrequens utriusque speciei usus fuisset tamen progressu temporis latissime iam mutata illa consuetudine gravibus et iustis causis adducta hanc consuetudinem sub altera specie communicandi approbavit et pro lege habendam decrevit quam reprobare aut sine ipsius Ecclesiae auctoritate pro libito mutare non licet."

pizza and coke.[12] Hence, there are limitations to papal authority regarding the administration of the sacraments and, as the subsequent chapters will show, over the liturgy.

[12] While this example seems ridiculous, a Jesuit priest attempted to do that very thing in the 1980s. Fr. Cornelius Buckley, S.J. was silenced for many years when he pointed this out publicly.

Chapter III: General Principles regarding Limitation of Papal Authority over the Liturgy

In the prior chapter, initial indications of the limitations on papal authority were presented, but now the limitations must be more directly discussed. The observation must be made that the intention of the subsequent chapters is not to detract from the authentic and legitimate authority of the pope over the matters of the liturgy, but to establish a better sense of precisely where his authority lies in relation to the liturgy. Even in light of *Traditionis Custodes*, there can be a tendency to restrict the pope in matters which he has legitimate authority, and other matters, where he does not, to extend his authority. Necessary distinctions are crucial to provide precision in these matters in order to preserve charity and the unity of the faithful.

One distinction that has made its way into the academic discussion of the matter is that of Fr. Karl Rahner. He notes that:[1]

> Imagine that the Pope, as supreme pastor of the Church, issued a decree today requiring all the uniate churches of the Near East to give up their Oriental liturgy and adopt the Latin rite.... The Pope would not exceed the competence of his jurisdictional primacy by such a decree, but the decree would be legally valid. But we can also pose an entirely different question. Would it be morally licit for the Pope to issue such a decree? Any reasonable man and any true Christian would have to answer "no."

In this quote, Rahner is making a distinction between the pope's authority and the moral use of that authority. This is a legitimate distinction in the wider and more general context of moral theology,

---

[1]The quote can be found here, together with citation: https://wdtprs.com/2021/07/what-the-mighty-jesuit-karl-rahner-would-say-said-about-suppressing-summorum-pontificum/

especially in relation to certain aspects of the virtue of prudence as it applies to the liturgy. Some theologians are observing this distinction in order to address whether certain liturgical changes or restrictions by the pope in recent years and decades are legitimate.

However, this distinction would not solve many issues of obedience regarding liturgical changes that a pope may make, which are abusive in regard to the exercise of his authority, if they fell within the legitimate bounds of his authority. Moreover, as will be seen shortly, this distinction is inadequate, given the statements of the Popes, Councils, and Magisterium itself regarding the matter, and a precise reading of those statements does not rest upon this distinction. In the end, this distinction will be seen to apply here only in certain respects, since other principles and distinctions will apply. Hence, several statements of the Church, saints, and theological writers throughout time will be discussed in order to parse out the applicable principles, which determine the *ad rem* of papal authority over the liturgy, *i.e.*, that there are restrictions on the very authority itself that the pope has over the liturgy.

I. Natural Law

It was noted in chapter one that the pope is bound by the Divine Positive Law and Natural Law regarding his authority over the liturgy. This essentially means that he does not have the authority to promulgate a liturgy or liturgical change that is contrary to the Divine Positive Law or the Natural Law.[2] In regard to the Natural Law, an example would be if the pope were to promulgate a liturgical change to an existing rite or promulgate a new rite which would contain something which was materially false. For to do so would result in the priest saying something during the liturgy which would be false, and

[2]Cf. Suarez, *De Fide*, X, VI, n. 16: "Si enim aliquid statuat contra bonos mores, non erit illi parendum ; si quidpiam tentet contra manifestam justitiam et commune bonum, fas erit illi resistere; si vim inferat, ejus in magnum vergeret Ecclesiæ detrimen vi poterit repelli, cum moderamine inculpatæ tutelea."

therefore, displeasing to God. If such a thing were to happen, that pope or a subsequent pope would be required to suppress that liturgy, or change or modify the liturgy in such a manner that it would not contain that liturgical element.[3]

II. Divine Positive Law

The observation that the pope's authority regarding the liturgy (as well as other matters) is limited or circumscribed by the Natural Law and Divine Positive Law is noted by more than one author. As Ludwig Ott observes:

> As the supreme lawgiver of the Church, the Pope is not legally bound by ecclesiastical decisions and usages, but by divine law alone. This demands that the papal power, in consonance with

---

[3]There are additional examples of this, but the most notable was the change made by Pope Benedict XVI to the words of consecration in certain languages. While the Latin version remained immune from the problem, certain languages, such as English, contained a line during the Consecration that was materially false. The original Latin of the Missal of Paul VI contained in Latin *pro multis,* which is what is contained in the Vulgate, while the English translation was rendered "for all." This led to some debate in some circles regarding the matter. Some argued that Christ did die for all in the Thomistic sense of sufficiency, even though as to efficacy, it extended to the many (see ST III, q .78, a.3, ad 8). The questions primarily revolved in the debate around validity, and most sided with St. Thomas that it did not render the *Novus Ordo Missae* invalid on that account. But the problem lies in the fact that Christ did *not* say "for all;" He said "for many." The priest according to the text was to say that Christ said "for all," but He did not. This constituted a material falsity in the text. While most priests would not intend any falsity in the matter, which is why it would remain in a vast majority of the cases as a material falsity, to promulgate a liturgical text with that falsity would constitute an objective violation of the Natural Law (8th Commandment) to not bear false witness. For this reason, Pope Benedict XVI was right in making the changes to the translation to bring it into conformity with what Christ actually said and what the Latin version actually contained. This would also help to avoid any universal salvationism, which could arise from a superficial understanding of the text and Revelation itself.

> its purpose, should be employed for the building-up of the Mystical Body of Christ, not for its destruction (2 Cor. 10:8). The divine law, therefore, is an efficacious brake on arbitrariness. The third Gallican article, which demanded a far-reaching limitation of the exercise of the Papal power, was properly rejected. D 1324.[4]

A few observations about this quote from Ott are in order. The pope is bound by the divine law, and since the divine law is distinguished between the Natural Law and the Divine Positive Law, the pope does not have the authority to introduce anything into the liturgy which is contrary to Revelation. In this sense, in making liturgical changes, the pope is bound by the Divine Positive Law. For example, the Pope would not have the authority to include as part of the canon a rejection of the divinity of Christ by asserting that God the Father alone was divine or something of this sort. In relation to the precepts in the New Testament, the pope could not, for example, forbid the priests and bishops from baptizing a certain group of people, since He said, "Going therefore, teach ye all nations: baptizing them in the name of the Father and of the Son and of the Holy Ghost."[5] While this does not touch on the liturgy itself, it does indicate that this part of Divine Positive Law binds the pope and can even restrict him in regard to his authority.

III. Authority as Part of Jurisdiction

After the Council of Trent, historically, several authors wrote on the question of papal authority over the liturgy. Very little was mentioned regarding the limitations other than what the Council of Trent had stated, as will be seen shortly. This was due in large part to the fact that they were often establishing the fact of his authority over

---

[4]Ott, *Fundamentals of Catholic Dogma*, p. 286.

[5]Matthew 28:19.

the liturgy contrary to Protestant objections. One work which is perhaps one of the most important theological texts during this time frame in regard to the question of the papal authority over the liturgy, is Bouix's *De Iure Liturgico*. In the text, he observes something which is also repeated by other authors, *viz.*, "the governance of the liturgy is an act of jurisdiction."[6] This one line contains a great deal that needs to be observed. The word governance which is *ordinatio* in Latin, which means to order, arrange, set in order, regulate, or ordain. It basically means that the authority which the Church has over the liturgy is one which includes the right to arrange, regulate or set in order certain matters. Arrange, regulate, or order by their nature indicate the right to govern, *i.e.*, to make determinations regarding the liturgy.

This right pertains to jurisdiction, which is defined as:

> *n.* **1**. the right to exercise official public authority in some capacity; rightful public power or its exercise in a perfect society. **2**. the territory within which some public authority may be lawfully exercised. **3**. the matters over which some public authority may be lawfully exercised.[7]

Jurisdiction, coming from the two Latin words *ius* and *dicere*, indicate that an authority has a "right to say," regarding a particular matter. This indicates that jurisdiction of the pope in regard to liturgical matters is a right that he has, but that right and authority is circumscribed by the Divine Positive Law and Natural Law, as has been seen. This is why "the power of *jurisdiction*...is immediately directed to ruling the faithful with reference to the attainment of life

---

[6]Bouix, *De Iure Liturgico*, p. 149 (and passim): "Liturgiae ordinatio est actus jurisdictionis."

[7]Wuellner, *A Dictionary of Scholastic Philosophy*, p. 157.

eternal."[8] Here, we see the proper matter of the jurisdiction of the pope in relation to the liturgy, *i.e.*, his authority is ultimately ordered toward the salvation of souls. Another way to express this reality would be that his authority is that which is outlined (*i.e.*, granted by Christ) and determined by what is revealed. Hence, while the pope does have authority over the liturgy, that authority is limited:

> The fullness of power (*plenitudo potestas*) of the Roman Pontiff is the power necessary to defend and promote the doctrine and discipline of the Church. It is not "absolute power" which would include the power to change doctrine or to eradicate liturgical discipline which has been alive in the Church since the time of Pope Gregory the Great and even earlier.[9]

The question as to whether the pope can abrogate a rite will be discussed in a later chapter. However, at this point, the main thing to see in the quote by Cardinal Burke is that the fullness of power does not mean absolute power. Fullness, in this theological context, indicates that it is supreme, *i.e.*, above all other forms of authority in the Church. It does not encompass the ability to deny or reject Revelation or the Divine Positive Law. To formulate it another way, the pope does not have the authority to introduce something into the liturgy which is contrary to the perennial and unchanging Deposit of Faith.[10] As per the above example, he would not have the authority to

---

[8]Parente, *Dictionary of Dogmatic Theology*, p. 124.

[9]Cardinal Raymond Burke as found in Kwasniewski, *From Benedict's Peace to Francis's War*, p. 118.

[10]Turcemata, *Summa de Ecclesia*, l. III, c. 57: "And it is clear that the pope can neither change nor revoke the articles of faith, nor the precepts of the law of nature, or the decalogue, nor the sacraments, just as nor can he dispense from them, and for this the meaning must be taken or understood." ("Et patet quod papa

introduce language that would deny Christ's divinity by asserting Arianism into the Canon of the Mass, which refers to God the Father alone as God to the exclusion of the other Persons of the Blessed Trinity.

IV. Tradition as a Norm

Since the Deposit of Faith comes via Sacred Tradition and Scripture, then even Sacred Tradition becomes a norm in regard to the papal authority over the liturgy. Hence, we read:

> The Pope is not an absolute monarch whose will is law, but is the guardian of the authentic Tradition, and thereby the premier guarantor of obedience. He cannot do as he likes, and is thereby able to oppose those people who for their part want to do what has come into their head. His rule is not that of arbitrary power, but that of obedience in faith. That is why, with respect to the Liturgy, he has the task of a gardener, not that of a technician who builds new machines and throws the old ones on the junk-pile. The "rite", that form of celebration and prayer which has ripened in the faith and the life of the Church, is a condensed form of living tradition in which the sphere which uses that rite expresses the whole of its faith and its prayer, and thus at the same time the fellowship of generations one with another becomes something we can experience, fellowship with the people who pray before us and after us. Thus the rite is something of benefit which is given to the Church, a living form of paradosis, the handing-on of

---

nec articulos fidei, nec praecepta legis naturae vel decalogi, aut sacramenta potest mutare sive revocare, sicut nec in illis potest dispensare, et ad istum sensus accipienda, sive intelligenda sunt...") Within the context of this quote is where Turcemata observes that papal authority must be for the utility of the Church.

> tradition.[11]

Here Cardinal Ratzinger is observing that the pope is a gardener, or we may say, a custodian of the liturgical rites as they come down to us via the tradition. The Cardinal further observes:

> Rites...are forms of the apostolic Tradition and of its unfolding in the great places of the Tradition.... After the Second Vatican Council, the impression arose that the pope really could do anything in liturgical matters.... The First Vatican Council had in no way defined the pope as an absolute monarch. On the contrary, it presented him as the guarantor of obedience to the revealed Word.... The authority of the pope is not unlimited; it is at the service of Sacred Tradition.[12]

The importance in regard to the Apostolic tradition will be seen in the subsequent chapter. What is important here is that papal authority in regard to the liturgy is one of service to the Sacred Tradition. Since the tradition has a binding force based upon what particular aspect of tradition one is addressing,[13] it is necessary, therefore, to make distinctions about the authority of the pope in relation to the liturgy. Obviously, he has authority and according to the Council of Trent, he can make changes to the liturgy, save the substance of the sacraments. But authors are pointing out that this distinction, while true, does not preclude certain restrictions on papal authority. Therefore, what

---

[11]Joseph Cardinal Ratzinger, Preface to Alcuin Reid, *The Organic Development of the Liturgy*, pp. 10-11.

[12]Cardinal Ratzinger as found in Kwasniewski, *From Benedict's Peace to Francis's War,* p. 31.

[13]See Ripperger, *Binding Force of Tradition; Magisterial Authority;* and *Consensus of the Fathers and Theologians.*

compromises the *lex orandi* is precisely the liturgical rites as they were initiated by the Apostles and slowly developed and were promulgated and approved through the tradition of the Church. At the root of this observation is that the Sacred Tradition of the Church constitutes a norm which guides and, in some circumstances, would restrict the pope's authority over the liturgy.

The pope is bound by prior decrees of councils and popes who enjoy infallibility as well as the consensus of the Theologians and the Fathers of the Church.[14] Due to the fact that the *lex credendi statuit lex supplicandi*,[15] the pope's authority over the liturgy is restricted by the formal teachings of the Church, *i.e.*, he is bound by elements of the tradition, which are part of the Deposit of Faith or which have been determined by the various organs of infallibility, etc. The liturgy from the time of the Apostles underwent a slow development as is evidenced in the historical documents and fragments, which contain the liturgical texts or parts, as well as testimony by the Fathers of the Church and the whole of the theological community throughout time in its observations about what was present in the liturgy at different times. This slow development was based upon the teachings contained in the Deposit of Faith as well as the various other theological sources or fonts. Since the faith did not change, certain elements of the liturgy simply never changed as a reflection of the unchanging *Depositum Fidei*. Furthermore, we also know by the liturgical texts that the change was slow, but generally contained what went before it. All of this indicates that certain aspects of the tradition are a norm for the pope's authority over the liturgy. By norm, we do not just mean that morally he is bound to follow the tradition, but also that his authority is restricted or limited based upon certain aspects of the tradition. For

---

[14]See Ripperger, *Magisterial Authority* and *Consensus of the Fathers and Theologians*.

[15]The reader is reminded also that Pope Pius XII observed that it is what is believed that determines the prayer.

example, he could not introduce into the liturgy a change which rejects the two-fold consecration of Mass. Such a change would be directly contrary to divine tradition as we see Christ in Scripture specifically saying, "do *this* in commemoration of me,"[16] that the "this" is clearly the offering of the Holy Sacrifice of the Mass containing a two-fold Consecration, one in which contains the transubstantiation of the bread into His Body (and Blood, Soul and Divinity) and the other contains the transubstantiation of the wine into His Blood (and Body, Soul and Divinity[17]).

Human nature and the Deposit of Faith, *i.e.*, Revelation, do not change. Hence, any authentic liturgical development would also develop organically, which is just another way of saying that certain elements remain the same, while others are augmented, allowed to flower, so to speak, and change. Organic is a term which implies that the substance of the thing remains, while accidental qualities change over time, as organic implies coming from a living organism, which remains the same organism in its substance as long as it is alive, despite undergoing accidental changes. Perhaps here is where we see so many difficulties arising. Due to systematic collapse of Thomistic or realist metaphysics in the Church, even the understanding of what constitutes a legitimate liturgical development has been impacted.[18]

Given the fact that the Deposit of Faith does not change and constitutes the *lex* around which the liturgical development hinged,

---

[16]Emphasis mine.

[17]That the other aspects of Christ are present when one of them is present is called real concomitance, see. ST III, q. 76. a. 1.

[18]Thomistic/realist metaphysics discovers the true principles that provide an understanding of substance, accidents, living being, and organic development. If these principles are rejected, ignored, or unknown, then the bankrupt contemporary theories of progressivism (neo-modernism) will necessarily fill the gap.

only an organic development can be legitimately envisioned.[19] To subject the liturgy to a major revision, which by its nature is not organic, would constitute a rejection of either (a) the unchangeableness of the Deposit of Faith, (b) unchanging human nature,[20] (c) the involvement of the Holy Spirit in the liturgical life of the Church for twenty centuries, or (d) the Apostolicity of certain elements of the liturgy.[21]

This is why in the documents of Vatican II, we read:

---

[19]Along these lines, see Massimo Viglione as found in Kwasniewski, *From Benedict's Peace to Francis's War,* p. 104: "The *lex orandi* of the Church, furthermore, is not a specific and determined 'thing' in time and space, as much as it is the collective whole of theological and spiritual norms and liturgical and pastoral practices of the entire history of the Church, from evangelical times – and specifically from Pentecost – up to today." Ibid., p. 105: "The *lex orandi* comprises all twenty centuries of the history of the Church, and there is no man or group of men in the world who can change this twenty-century-old deposit. There is no pope, council, or episcopate that can change the Gospel, the *Depositum Fidei*, or the universal Magisterium of the Church. Nor can the Liturgy of all time be [decisively] changed."

[20]The idea that modern man was fundamentally different than his predecessors, and therefore, needed a completely different rite or form of the Mass, has no basis in realist metaphysics or the doctrine of original sin. If anything, the mass murders by heads of state during the 1930s-1950s, including, Hitler, Mao and Stalin, were a sign that man had not changed at all and was just as prone to sin as his forefathers, and therefore, needed redemption as much as his ancestors. The fact that the liturgy emphasized man's sinfulness, his need for redemption, that Christ alone saves, etc., was needed at the very time the call for reform was being made. What really needed reform, without denying the ability of the liturgy to continue to organically develop, was the generation alive when the reforms were called for. If anything, WWII and its aftermath showed that man, being under the effects of original and actual sin, had not changed at all. What was needed was serious action on the side of the Church to reform its members.

[21]See subsequent chapter.

> That sound tradition may be retained, and nevertheless the way of legitimate progress may be opened, accurate theological, historical and pastoral investigation of the particular known parts of the Liturgy is always to precede.[22]

This passage poses many things for consideration. It is not clear that a sound tradition was maintained. If it were so, it would have been organic in its nature and the variation would have probably looked more like the Missals that were promulgated in 1965 and 1967. It may even be argued that these were not well done either, but at least the liturgical development would have looked more like what was actually contained in the document of *Sacrosanctum Concilium*. Regardless, what appears to have occurred was not a reflection of the tradition in the subsequent developments.

This is why the document often referred to as the papal oath observed:

> To keep the discipline and rite of the Church, as I have found it, and as I discovered it given by my Holy predecessors, inviolable. ...To keep the discipline and the rite, as we find it canonically handed down by my holy predecessors, as long as life is in them.[23]

---

[22]Vatican II, *Sacrosanctum Concilium*, para. 23: "Ut sana traditio retineatur et tamen via legitimae progressioni aperiatur, de singulis Liturgiae partibus recognoscendis accurata investigatio theologica, historica, pastoralis semper praecedat."

[23]*Patrologia Latina*, 105, 42C (Liber Diurnus Romanorum Pontificum, Lib. II, Titulum VII): "Disciplinam et ritum Ecclesiae, sicut inveni, et a Sanctis praecessoribus meis traditum reperi, inlibatum custodire; [second column]: "Disciplinam et ritum, sicut invenimus a Sanctis praedecessoribus meis canonice traditum, quamdiu vita in istis comes fuerit, illibate custodire." See also Pope Innocent I in his letter to Bishop Gubbio (PL 20: 552) regarding guarding or holding the traditions held by all.

The pope, even in matters of the liturgy, was bound to "hold fast to the traditions."[24]

V. Heretics and the Liturgy

A consistent problem throughout the history of the Church has been precisely that those who do not hold to the traditions of the Church seek to change the liturgy. To put it more succinctly, "the striving of heretics is to corrupt the liturgy."[25] In a longer explanation, Vacante, in the *Dictionnaire de Théologie Catholique,* states:

> Heretics and Alterations of the Liturgy. – We can give another proof of the dogmatic importance of the liturgy, it is that most heretics began by altering it to make it conform to their errors and that the Church was obliged to condemn these efforts. This paragraph is therefore a complement to the previous one in that it shows the Magisterium of the Church exercising itself against these endeavors.[26]

Three items should be observed in this quote. The first is that heretics immediately begin the process of changing the liturgy to conform to their errors. This is a general pattern shown throughout the entire

---

[24]2 Thes. 2:15.

[25]Oppenheim, *Institutiones Systematico-Historica in Sacram Liturgiam*, Vol. VII, *Principia Theologiae Liturgiae*, p. 59: "Haereticorum Nisus corrumpendi Liturgiam."

[26]Vacant, *Dictionnaire de Théologie Catholique*, vol. IX, p. 839: "IX. Les Hérétiques et les Altérations de la Liturgie. – On peut donner une autre preuve de l'importance dogmatique de la liturgie, c'est que la plupart des hérétiques commencèrent par l'altérer pour la rendre conforme à leurs erreurs et que l'Église fut obligée de condamner ces efforts. Ce paragraphe est donc un complément du précédent en ce qu'il montre le magistère de l'Église s'exerçant contre ces entreprises."

history of the Church. Psychologically, this stands to reason as the liturgy as it organically developed throughout time was an expression of the very faith that the heretics rejected. It is for this reason that Pope Gregory XVI made the following observation:

> As we have the opportunity of writing you, we cannot refrain from indicating to you another point that requires particular vigilance on the part of your Fraternity: especially those very priests whom we have already mentioned above who, taken in by novelty, do not fear to undervalue sacred rites and criticize the venerable usages of the Church, nor spare any effort to induce you, Venerable Brother, to publish a new Ritual that will satisfy their desires. But, conscious of your duty, watch constantly over the institutions of the ancient and never allow your clergy to depart from any prescription of the Ritual of the Holy Roman Church or from any rule that may have been inserted in any other Ritual you use, provided that the Ritual be ancient and approved by the lawful authority. We trust, Venerable Brother, that you will take this advice to heart in all obedience; and knowing that there have been changes in this field, we exhort and beseech you in our Lord not to delay in suppressing and correcting the innovations introduced. Heretics seek to change liturgy so the pope as a matter of prudence must not seek to make changes except under certain circumstances; he must watch over it and guard it.[27]

---

[27]Gregory XVI, (as found in *The Liturgy*) Letter Dolorem, quo jam diu, November 30, 1839, to the Bishop of Fribourg, p. 119. See also Council of Trent, Sess. XXII: "Sacrosancta oecumenica et generalis Tridentina synodus in spiritu sancto legitime congregata praesidentibus in ea eisdem apostolicae sedis legatis: ut vetus absoluta atque omni ex parte perfecta de magno eucharistiae mysterio in sancta catholica ecclesia fides atque doctrina retineatur et in sua puritate propulsatis erroribus atque haeresibus conservetur: de ea quatenus verum et singulare sacrificium est spiritus sancti illustratione edocta haec quae sequuntur docet declarat et fidelibus populis praedicanda decernit." ("That the ancient,

Pope Gregory is observing that one must be on guard against novelty. In fact, we can say that novelty introduced into the liturgy would in most cases be a red flag. Here we are not talking about an introduction of an element that has heretofore not been in the liturgy, but a new element which seems to be at variance with the tradition, as the pope says above. Again, heretics seek to change the liturgy, which is why historically, the development of the liturgy was always organic,[28] so as not to depart from sound tradition, as Vatican II observes. It is also why the changes were made slowly, only one or two minor adjustments being made, here or there as a general rule, rather than wholesale change which gives the impression of novelty, *i.e.*, a change in the faith, which heretics seek.

This is connected to the second observation from the prior quote and it was also noted in the quote by Pope Gregory, *viz.*, the obligation of the pope to (a) keep watch over the liturgy to make sure its religious integrity is preserved, but (b) also that prudence is observed that he must not seek to change it, except under certain circumstances. The latter constitutes a limitation on the pope insofar as he is morally bound by the virtue of prudence, and actions contrary to prudence are sinful.[29] In other words, it is contrary to the Natural Law or Divine Positive Law for the pope to make changes that are contrary to prudence. It would seem, therefore, if Pope Gregory's

---

complete and in every way perfect faith and teaching regarding the great mystery of the Eucharist in the Catholic Church may be retained, and with the removal of errors and heresies may be preserved in its purity, the holy, ecumenical and general Council of Trent, lawfully assembled in the Holy Ghost, the same legates of the Apostolic See presiding, instructed by the light of the Holy Ghost, teaches, declares and orders to be preached to the faithful the following concerning it, since it is the true and only sacrifice.")

[28]An organic development is one in which the substance of the liturgy remains intact, preserving the integrity of the ancient liturgy doctrine.

[29]See chapter five.

observation is correct, that for a pope to make sweeping wholesale changes would be contrary to prudence, and therefore, contrary to the Divine Positive Law and the Natural Law, at least in relation to prudence.

Morever, the pope has to ensure that the integrity of the liturgy is maintained, so that the faith which is manifested in the liturgy is truly Catholic. The pope is a custodian of the liturgy, but he is also to "confirm the brethren."[30] This is a direct command given by God (Christ) to St. Peter (and his successors). Part of the Divine Positive Law that is incumbent on the pope specifically is that he must never do anything contrary to that command and must actively seek to strengthen the faith, virtue, and sanctity of the members of the Church. Hence, any liturgical change which would cause scandal, militate against the virtue of faith of the faithful, or favor heresy, not in its essential content, but as to its overall effect on the Church, would be outside the authority of the pope, since his authority is circumscribed by the Divine Positive Law.

The third item concerning the quote above is that the liturgy cannot militate against the faith of the faithful, but is ultimately a form of intellectual formation. In other words, what people see in the liturgy tells them what we believe. Hence, "although the sacred Liturgy specifically pertains to the cult of the divine majesty, it also contains great erudition of the faithful people."[31] Anything that is contrary to the right education and formation of the faithful intellectually or spiritually is not within the jurisdiction of the pope.[32]

---

[30]Luke 22:32.

[31]Vatican II, *Sacrosanctum Concilium*, para. 33: "Etsi sacra Liturgia est praecipue cultus divinae maiestatis, magnam etiam continent populi fidelis eruditionem."

[32]This may not be immediately evident, but would be seen in its fruits. For example, the collapse in the faith over the past 60 years is evident. It would appear, in that respect, that the changes were not prudent for the formation of the

VI. Longevity

One of the ways to discern the Will of God regarding some element of the liturgy is by determining how long it has been part of the liturgy. While one can consider the source of the liturgical element, such as Our Lord, the Apostles, a pope or a saint, in having some sense of the Will of God regarding that element, how long something has been known to be in the liturgy itself can give one an indicator of God's will regarding it.

> It is able to occur that some end or use *for some time* is found in the liturgy, which is not in congruity with the truth after it is defined or after it is commonly, as well as certainly acknowledged, or that the opinions regarding it allow for sometime, which are debated; for the live doctrine is prior to the theory in practice; and this especially as long as the Church has not given in belief (*sententiam*) on the matter. And such end or use remains for a time in liturgical practice, until it is authentically corrected in the respective liturgical books. Nevertheless, excluded in the liturgy in a forceful way at the same time something which is opposed to the doctrine of the Church.[33]

faithful.

[33]Oppenheim, *Institutiones Systematico-Historica in Sacram Liturgiam*, Vol. VII, Principia Theologiae Liturgiae, p. 73: "Fieri potest ut aliquis terminus vel usus aliquando *per aliquod tempus* in Liturgiae inveniatur, qui non congruit cum veritate postea definita vel postea communiter tamquam certa agnita, vel ut opiniones in ea aliquandiu sinantur, quae discutiuntur; vita enim doctrina est prior, praxis theoria; et hoc praesertim tamdiu, quamdiu Ecclesia nondum clare suam de re sententiam dedit. Et talis terminus vel usus interdum ad tempus manet in praxi liturgica, usquedum in revisione respectivi libri liturgici authentice corrigatur. Verumtamen excluditur in Liturgia modo in vigore aliquid inveniri, quod opponitur doctrinae Ecclesiae eiusdem temporis."

This passage needs careful unpacking. Oppenhiem is reflecting the general consensus of authors that something can make its way into the liturgy that is contrary to the teaching of the Church. While normally this would be a topic which is still open for discussion, once the Church decides on the matter, then it may take some time to be removed from the liturgical books, *i.e.*, it may not occur until the next set of liturgical books are updated.

What is underlying this observation is that since the Church is established to give God rightly ordered worship, anything that is disordered or displeasing to God will eventually be removed from the liturgy of the Church. It does not mean that, during a time of heresy, erroneous or disordered elements will not work their way into the liturgy, but that eventually God will move the pope or rightful authorities to remove those elements that are contrary to the Catholic Faith. Hence, the principle that undergirds this process is that God keeps watch over the liturgy and moves the pope or rightful authorities to remove those things which do not please Him.

The converse of this, therefore, also obtains. Due to the fact that God is the Lord of History, that He established the Church to give Him rightly ordered worship, so much so that He gave detailed instructions,[34] nothing remains in the liturgy *over a long period of time* that is not the Will of God that it be there. From this, the principle is that the longevity of an element of the liturgy gives indication of the Will of God regarding that element. To formulate it another way, how long something is in the liturgical books determines how much God wants that in the liturgy.[35] If something is from

---

[34]See next section.

[35]Longevity would be distinct from antiquity insofar as something could have longevity, *e.g.*, be in the liturgy for 400 years but it would not have antiquity, since it does not date to the time of the Apostles or Early Church. Hence, every element that enjoys antiquity also enjoys longevity, but not every element that enjoys longevity enjoys antiquity.

Apostolic tradition, this indicates that God generally wants that element in the liturgy for the entire duration of the Church's history. If it is introduced very early on and has remained in the liturgy of the Church for 1400 years, as is the case of the liturgy codified by Pope Gregory the Great, that is generally an indicator that God wants it to continue in the life of the Church. Otherwise, He would move the pope or rightful authorities to remove it beforehand, because it would not be His will, and He would not delay for 1400 years. Hence, the longer something is in the liturgy, as is evidenced by the extant liturgical texts throughout history, the more it is the Will of God that this element be in the liturgy.

This would indicate that when a pope is contemplating a liturgical change, he must take into consideration the longevity of the particular liturgical element in the liturgy in order to be rightly said to be observing the Will of God. If God had kept an element in the liturgy almost from the beginning of the Church, or even for 1400 years, it is difficult to see where there would be any justification for that change. Since human nature and the Deposit of Faith do not change, the longevity of an element of the liturgy for a very long period of time indicates that the liturgical element in question is in congruity with the Divine Positive Law and the Natural Law and takes human nature as laboring under original sin into proper consideration.

It is precisely the longevity that inspires, not just Fear of the Lord, but also true piety in those who have made liturgical changes over the course of time. Fear of the Lord is fear of offending God by what we do, and so liturgical changes that had longevity demonstrated the Will of God regarding the matter. Consequently, there was generally a "hands off" approach to those elements so as not to offend God. But true piety was also part of the consideration. Piety is the reverence and honor that we give to our parents, in the proper sense.[36] By extension, piety is the reverence we have for our parents in the

---

[36]ST II-II, q. 101, a. 1.

faith, *i.e.*, our forefathers in the faith. As the forefathers are known for their greatness, especially in relation to the liturgy, then great care is to be taken in considering any change to the elements of the liturgy which they begot. In the Roman Rite, this would include great saints such as St. Gregory the Great and St. Pius V. In the eastern rites, this would include St. John Chrysostom, St. Basil, and Gregory Nazinazen.[37] It would be sheer impiety to simply jettison hundreds of years of liturgical development and codification of the liturgy based upon one's perception of one's own times. Yet, this is exactly what the Catholic Church saw the Protestants do when they changed the liturgy. No forefather or his contribution was immune from being trampled underfoot.[38]

VII. Exactitude in the Worship of God

Pope Pius XII in *Mediator Dei* makes the following observation:

> Thus we observe that when God institutes the Old Law, He makes provision besides for sacred rites, and determines in exact detail the rules to be observed by His people in rendering Him the worship He ordains. To this end He established various kinds of sacrifice and designated the ceremonies with which they were to be offered to Him. His enactments on all matters relating to the Ark of the Covenant, the Temple and the holy days are minute and clear. He established a sacerdotal tribe with its high priest, selected and described the vestments with which the sacred ministers were to be clothed, and every function in any way pertaining to divine worship. Yet this was nothing more than a faint foreshadowing of the worship which the High Priest of the

---

[37]This is why Latinization of the eastern rites is particularly concerning.

[38]See Davies, *Cramner's Godly Order.*

New Testament was to render to the Father in heaven.[39]

What the pope is saying is that when it comes to worshiping God, God gives minute and exacting details in how it is to be done. This is clearly demonstrated in the Old Testament in the Book of Exodus where God gives detailed instructions regarding the rituals to the Jews.[40]

Why did he give such detailed instructions? The reason is clear historically and is evident even today. To order a means to the end, the means must be proportionate to the end.[41] God is the end of worship and so in order to know how to order the means to the end, one must have a right knowledge of the end. But during the time of the Jews, the knowledge of God was inchoate. While philosophy, specifically metaphysics as natural theology, can have a knowledge of God, it is not adequate and is prone to many errors regarding God.[42] If we get the end wrong, the means will inevitably be wrong. Hence, without God revealing Himself, our worship of Him will end up disordered, because of the defects of original sin of darkness of the intellect and disordered appetites.

---

[39]Pius XII, *Mediator Dei*, para.16: "Itaque, si Deum consideramus veterem condentem legem, eum cernimus de sacris etiam ritibus edere praecepta, accuratasque decernere normas, quibus populus obtemperet in legitimo eidem praestando cultu. Quamobrem varia statuit sacrificia, variasque designavit caerimonias, quibus dicatum sibi munus offerretur; eaque omnia perspicue significavit, quae ad foederis arcam, ad templum, ad diesque festos pertinerent. Sacerdotalem tribum et summum sacerdotem constituit; ac vestes etiam indicavit ac descripsit, quibus sacrorum administri uterentur, et quidquid aliud praeterea ad divinum cultum respiceret."

[40]Exodus 24-31.

[41]See chapter on prudence.

[42]This is why St. Thomas says Revelation is necessary, see ST I, q. 1, a. 1.

Yet, even if we know the right things about God, human beings are so prone to error that it is not reasonable to expect them to know how to arrive at the right means to the end. In other words, if you look at the various forms of pagan worship, etc., in the Old Testament, it is clear that they know not God, nor how to worship Him. Even when the Jews knew about God, they deviated into certain forms of worship that were displeasing to Him, by falling into worship of other religions at times. This is why in the end God must reveal the proper rituals in which to worship Him and He must keep vigilance over those rituals by means of the graces given to the Magisterium and on the part of the Tradition, in order to keep out of the worship anything that is disordered.

Pope Pius XII also observed that the exactitude given to the Jews in the Old Testament is just a foreshadowing of what Christ gave in the New Testament. Christ Himself said, "do *this* in commemoration of me." As will be seen in a subsequent chapter, He also gave certain detailed instructions about the liturgy according to the Fathers of the Church. Then He fashioned the liturgy over the course of time, as was discussed in the section on longevity. It is for these reasons that any contemplated liturgical changes must take into consideration the exactitude that has occurred in the liturgy from the time of Christ on. Since God prunes the liturgy like a tree, it is precisely for this reason that the men who should be entrusted with that work can only be the saints, or those with grace of office who have demonstrated fidelity to that grace,[43] since they alone know the mind of God, have a deep Fear of the Lord, and will be very careful and exact in the changes proposed.

VIII. A Necessary Distinction

The Council of Trent makes the following observation which is referenced more than once in this work due to its importance in the

---

[43]See De Mattei, *Saint Pius V*, p. 312.

context of this discussion:

> It declares furthermore, that in the dispensation of the sacraments, "salva illorum substantia," the Church may, according to circumstances, times and places, determine or change whatever she may judge most expedient for the benefit of those receiving them or for the veneration of the sacraments; and this power has always been hers.[44]

This passage essentially shows that the Church has authority to change the liturgy "except those which pertain to the substance" of the sacraments. Historically, this has led to many theologians asserting that except for those things necessary for the validity of the sacraments, the Church had the authority to change it, and this would include the pope. Among those theologians are Suarez,[45] St. Alphonsus Ligouri,[46] the Salamancan Fathers,[47] Franzelin,[48] and Kendrick.[49] This would primarily pertain to the essence of the

---

[44]Council of Trent, Session XXII, c. 7 (Denz. 931): "Praeterea declarat hanc potestatem perpetuo in ecclesia fuisse ut in sacramentorum dispensatione salva illorum substantia ea statueret vel mutaret quae suscipientium utilitati seu ipsorum sacramentorum venerationi pro rerum temporum et locorum varietate magis expedire iudicaret."

[45]*De Sacramentis*, d. XV, s. iii, (Comm. in III D. Thomae, tom. III). See also *De legibus* lib. IV, cap. iv, n. 14; *De sacramentis*, d. LXXIV, s. iii and *Defensio fidei*, l. IV, c. ix, n. 26.

[46]*Opera dogmatica contra gli eretici pretesi riformati*, s. VII, n. 34 (Cf. Walter's Latin edition of his dogmatical works, Tom. I, p. 542).

[47]*De sacramentis in genere*, disp. X, d. I, p. 1, n. 1-4.

[48]*Tractatus de Sacramentis*, p. 187.

[49]*Theologia Dogmatica*, vol. 1, p. 252.

sacrament, including the matter and form. It is virtually impossible to find any authentic Catholic theologian who holds that the substance or essence of the sacraments which include the matter and form can be other than they are without invaliding the sacrament. However, for purposes of showing its continuity in the tradition, we see the theological treatises dealing with the essential matter and form in the writings of Pope Clement VI,[50] Pope Eugene IV,[51] St. Thomas Aquinas,[52] the Council of Trent,[53] Suarez,[54] St. Robert Bellarmine,[55] Pope Leo XIII,[56] Pope Pius X,[57] and Cardinal Billot,[58] just to name a few.

The pope would not have the authority to change the matter of the sacraments, *e.g.*, he would not be able to change the matter of the Eucharist to rice patties for the Body or to whiskey for the Blood of Our Lord. He would not have the authority to change the matter of Baptism to a sanitizing gel, despite the fact that it might cleanse in some superficial manner the one being baptized: it must be water. The pope would also not have the authority to promulgate a rite of Mass in which the words of consecration were altered to invalidate the

---

[50]*Super quibusdam (Decimo).*

[51]*Exsultate Deo* at the Council of Florence (*Quinto*).

[52]ST III, q. 60 and ibid., q. 66, a. 10.

[53]As just noted above but also Session XIV, c. 2.

[54]*De sacramentis*, disp. II.

[55]*De sacramentis in genere*, lib. I, c. xviii-xxi.

[56]*Apostolicae curae*, para. 24 (Denz. 1963).

[57]Pius X, *Ex quo* (Denz. 3035).

[58]*De Ecclesiae sacramentis*, q. LX, thes. I-II.

Mass. For example, he could not change the words of consecration to, "this is my person," or "this is like my Blood." The entire theological tradition has held that certain words for the Eucharist are absolutely necessary for validity, and therefore, the pope cannot change those essential words. He also may not introduce words that substantially change the meaning of the form, as was just noted in using the word "like" in relation to His Blood. It is not "like" His Blood, since this indicates it is a different substance that is similar to His Blood, but not actually His Blood.

Moreover, the pope would not have the authority to promulgate a rite of Mass in which there are no words of consecration. This is due to the fact that the form of the sacrament indicates the *vis sacramenti,*[59] which is the very thing that brings the sacrament into existence. Without the essential words of consecration, then even if the entire canon is "euchological" in the sense of referring to Our Lord, as some suggest, unless the words themselves have the sense of the actual substance of the sacrament, then no sacrament occurs, regardless of how much verbiage is in the prayer. When the priest says the words of Consecration, it is precisely his saying those specific words that has the force of the sacrament (*vis sacramenti*). Thus, it is said that the priest actually *commands* the sacrament to be present[60] and a command is done by a specific set of words. Any

---

[59]ST III, q. 76, a. 1.

[60]This follows from several principles. The first is that the sacraments work *ex opere operato* and not *ex opere operantis*. If the sacraments worked *ex opere operantis*, it would be based on the merit of the minister, which means that sometimes the sacraments would occur and sometimes they would not. Whereas, because the sacraments work *ex opere operato*, they do so because once the form is pronounced over the proper matter and the intention of minister is to confect the sacrament, then the sacrament occurs. To put this another way, when the minister uses his will to pronounce the words according to his intention, he is commanding the sacrament to be present, at least in relation to those things that pertain to the priesthood. Since the indellible mark is a power (*potestas* – see ST III, q., 63, a.

human being knows this intuitively; *e.g.*, if someone approaches him and begins talking about the need of a hole to be dug, how the hole is important, how the hole will make it possible to put up the flag pole, how the hole needs to be a certain size, etc., that is entirely different than commanding him to "dig the hole." For all the individual knows, the other one is simply informing him, not telling him to dig the hole. Prayer begets what it signifies. If the priest does not command the sacrament to be present, but simply talks about it, even in the context of a prayer, then the sacrament does not occur. If it were the case that talking about the Eucharist but never saying the words of Consecration begot the sacrament, then any priest sitting in a bakery would need to avoid talking about the Eucharist, especially if he has a habitual intention of confecting the Eucharist whenever he talks about it.[61]

---

2) in the priest, he can command the sacraments to be present, as in the case of the Eucharist when he says the words. In effect, he is commanding the bread and wine by the power of his indellible mark (through which God Who is omnipotent works) to convert into the Body and Blood of Our Lord. One of the reasons for the priest commanding the sacrament to occur (imprecatory as opposed to deprecatory prayer) is the very notion of the *vis sacramenti*. The *vis sacramenti* is the very force of the sacrament, so when the priest says (commands) the form, the Body and Blood become present by the force of the sacrament.

[61]While this discussion seems like an academic exercise, it is a reality in recent years. On the 20th of July 2001, a document of the Holy See, titled *Guidelines for Admission to the Eucharist between the Chaldean Church and the Assyrian Church of the East*, drew the following conclusions from the recognition of the validity of the Holy Qurbana of Addai and Mari as celebrated in the Assyrian Church of the East: "Assyrian faithful are permitted, when necessary, to participate and to receive Holy Communion in a Chaldean celebration of the Holy Eucharist. Chaldean faithful unable to approach a Catholic minister are permitted to participate and to receive Holy Communion in an Assyrian celebration of the Holy Eucharist, even if celebrated using the Anaphora of Addai and Mari in its form without the Words of Institution. Assyrian ministers are warmly invited (but not obliged) to insert the Words of Institution in the Anaphora of Addai and Mari when Chaldean faithful are present at the liturgy." These guidelines were

The passage from the Council of Trent in which it says that the Church has the power to make changes to the rites save that which pertains to the substance is also interpreted slightly differently than just pertaining to what constitutes validity for the sacraments, *i.e.*, their matter and form. The first quote to begin this discussion is from Pope Pius XII:

> The sacred liturgy does, in fact, include divine as well as human elements. The former, instituted as they have been by God, cannot be changed in any way by men. But the human components admit of various modifications, as the needs of the age, circumstance and the good of souls may require, and as the ecclesiastical hierarchy, under guidance of the Holy Spirit, may have authorized; this pertains to apostolic tradition.[62]

This passage is very important for the following reasons. The first is that the Pope is observing that if something is of divine tradition, *i.e.*, given to us by God (Jesus Christ), then it cannot be changed in any way by men. As will be seen in a subsequent chapter, there are elements of the liturgy, which are of divine tradition, coming from Christ according to the Fathers, which do not pertain to the substance of the sacraments in respect to their validity alone. But the main thing here is to note that matters pertaining to divine tradition are outside the authority of the pope to change.

---

promulgated by the Pontifical Council for Promoting Christian Unity, therefore, they do not enjoy infalliblity.

[62]Pius XII, *Mediator Dei*, para. 50: "Sacra enim Liturgia ut humanis, ita divinis constat elementis; haec autem, ut patet, cum a Divino Redemptore constituta, fuerint, nullo modo ab hominibus mutari possunt; illa vero, prout temporum, rerum animorumque necessitates postulant, varias commutationes habere possunt, quas Ecclesiastica Hierarchia, S. Spiritus auxilio innixa, comprobaverit."

The second is precisely the reality that there are certain elements in the liturgy, particularly in the liturgy of the Mass, which are outside the authority of the pope to change, even though they do not touch upon the substance of the sacrament as such. This distinction is actually observed in some of the writers after Trent, that is, the distinction between what pertains to the substance of the sacraments, as such, (*i.e.*, the matter and form), and other elements in the liturgy that are outside the scope of the authority of the pope to change. One such author is Paolo Maria Quarto (or Quarti), the author of an influential rubrical commentary upon the *Missale Romanum,* who was regularly cited as an authority by Benedict XIV and other theologians and liturgists on rubrical and other liturgical matters. He writes:

> The Rites of the Mass are divided commonly into the essential, which are of the necessity of the sacrifice and of the Sacrament: and the accidental, which pertain to the ornament of the same sacrifice, and are able to be of necessity of precept, but not of the Sacrament. The essential Rite of the Mass consists in the consecration, indeed also the Communion, as we shall explain at greater length in the appendix of this work, when we discuss the sacrifice of the Mass, and [this essential Rite] descends from the institution of Christ the Lord. But the accidental Rite consists in the actions, and prayers, and other circumstances adjoined by the Church, which are called *Sacramentalia*, and Sacred Ceremonies. ...Ceremony is commonly taken for the accidental rite, and can be described thus. It is an external Religious action instituted by the Church for the worship and becomingness of the sacrifice, thus Suarez disput. 15, sec. 1, *ex his*, with the others cited above. The Sacred Ceremonies or *Sacramentalia*, therefore, agree with the Sacraments and the sacrifice in this, that they are external acts of the virtue of religion: but they differ insofar as the sacrifice contains the supreme worship of

God, unto a sign of the supreme excellence of God; the Sacraments are also ordered to the sanctification of the faithful through the infusion of habitual grace. But the *sacramentalia* and Ceremonies are ordered to the becoming mode of offering the sacrifice, of which they are accidental circumstances, nor do they have the power of infusing grace: thus Suarez, and the other Authors cited above. ...The Ceremonies can be divided firstly into those which are intrinsic to the Mass itself, and its parts: and they consist of the words and deeds of the celebrant, concerning which Suarez at length disput. 83 and 84, and Aversa compendiously in the place cited; and into those which are circumstances extrinsic to the same sacrifice, such as the place, time, vessels, and sacred vestments, about which we shall speak explicitly in their place. Secondly, the Ceremonies which consist in deeds, some have been introduced for the sake of the becomingness of the thing to be done, and have no other signification. For example, that the Priest, when he signs himself, places his left hand over his breast.[63]

---

[63]*Rubricae Missalis Romani commentariis illustratae quaest. fund.*, s. I, p. 2.: "Ritus Missae dividuntur communiter in essentiales, qui sunt de necessitate Sacrificii, et Sacramenti: et acccidentales, qui pertinent ad ornatum eiusdem Sacrificii, et possunt esse de necessitate praecepti, non vero Sacramenti. Ritus essentialis Missae consistit in Consecatione, vel etiam Communione, ut susius explicabimus in appendice hujus operis, dum de Sacrificio Missae: et oritur ex instituntione Christi Domini. Ritus vero accdentalis consistit in actionibus, et precibus, aliisque circumstantiis ab Eccleasia adjunctis, quae dicuntur Sacramentalia, et caeromonia sacrae... Caermonia communiter sumitur pro ritus accidentali, et potest ita describi: est action Religiosa externa, ad cultum et decentiam Sacrificii, ab Ecclesia instituta: ita Suarez disputat.15, sect. I *ex his*, com aliss supra citatis. Sacrae ergo caermoniae, seu Sacramentalia conveniunt cum Sacrements et Sacrificio in hoc, quod sunt actus externi virtutis Religionis: different vero, quod Sacrificium continent supremum Dei cultum, in signum supremae Dei excellentiae: Sacramenta ordinantury ad sancticationem fidelium per infusionem gratiae habitualis; at vero Sacramentalia, et Caermoniae

A very close reading of this rather lengthy citation yields the following observation. Paolo is observing a necessary distinction when referring to the *sacramentalia*, *viz.*, those things which pertain not just to the substance of the sacraments, but also to the necessity of the sacrifice.[64]

This would stand to reason. The essence of the *sacrifice* of the Mass does not just consist in the form and matter of the *sacrament*. In fact, it includes three essential elements, *viz.*, the Offertory,[65] the Canon (most specifically the slaying of the victim) and the

---

ordinantury ad decentem modum offerendi Sacrificium, cujus sunt circumstantiae accidentlais, nec habent virtutem infundendi gratiamL ita Suarez, et alii Auctores supra citati. Sacramenta ordinantury ad sancticationem fidelium per infusionem gratiae habitualis; at vero Sacramentalia, et Caermoniae ordinantury ad decentem modum offerendi Sacrificium, cujus sunt circumstantiae accidentlais, nec habent virtutem infundendi gratiamL ita Suarez, et alii Auctores supra citati. Dividi possunt Cacremoniae primo in eas quae sunt intrinsicae ipsi Missae, et partes eiusdem: et consistun tum in verbis, tum in gestibus celebrantis, de quibus at Suarez disp. 8, sect. 84, et compnedise Aversa loco supra citato. Et in ease quae sunt circumstantiae extrinsicae euisdem Sacrifcii, ut locus, tempus, vasa, et vestimenta sacra, de quibus suo loco ex prfesso dicemus. Secundo, Caermoniae quau consistun in gestibus, quaeda unductae sunt propter decentiam operandi, nec habent aliam significaitonem,: e.g. Quod Sacerdos dum signisse ipisum, ponit sinistram sub pectore."

[64]This distinction is also seen in the French Jesuit Val re Regnault *Praxis fori poenitentialis*, l. XXVI, c. iv, nn. 27-29. As Hurter's *Nomenclator literarius* notes, both St. Charles Borromeo and St. Francis de Sales commended his works to their clergy, and St. Alphonsus Ligouri in his *Theologia Moralis* numbered him amongst the authors of theology to be preferred most of all for their authority.

[65]Spirago, *The Catechism Explained*, p. 537: "There are three distinct parts in the sacrifice of the Mass: the offertory, the consecration, and the communion." Ibid., p. 536: "What takes place in the sacrifice of the Mass is this: the priest at the altar, as the representative of Christ, offers of bread and wine to Almighty God; he changes these substances into the body and blood of Christ, and destroys them by consuming them."

Communion of the priest.[66] As to the Offertory, if a ritual of the Mass did not contain a proper offertory, then it would be a meal in the proper sense. For what distinguishes a meal from a sacrifice is precisely the Offertory. If a person slays a victim and eats it, without dedicating it or consecrating it to God by an Offertory, that is what constitutes a meal. Whereas, once the Offertory is done, the *oblata* are set aside from profane use and its primary end is no longer to satisfy the one who eats it, even though that may occur. Rather, the *oblata* are now destined to be slain and consumed precisely for the worship of God and His pleasure. Even though the Holy Sacrifice of the Mass retains elements of a meal by having a slaying of victim and a consummation, these elements are no longer viewed under that aspect, once the Offertory is done, because the fulfillment of the creature in the consuming of the victim is no longer the primary end.

In fact, every single form of authentic sacrifice has these three elements, which is seen in the Old Testament and in the New Testament. Even Christ in His sacrifice upon Calvary had these three elements. The Offertory was at the Mount of Olives: "Father, if thou wilt, remove this chalice from me: but yet not my will, but thine be done."[67] Christ then underwent the brutal passion and died (slaying of

---

[66]Con Cochem, *The Incredible Catholic Mass*, p. 440: "The first essential part of Holy Mass: the Offertory" and p. 443: "The second essential part of Holy Mass: the Consecration" and p. 447: "The third essential part of Holy Mass: the Communion." Spirago, *The Catechism Explained*, p. 533: "The sacrifice is not consummated until the species of bread and wine are consumed." Crofts, *The Fullnes of Sacrifice*, p 171: Looking back over the ancient rituals of God's chosen people, which foreshadow the great things which were to come, we see that in nearly all these typical sacrifices there took place a consuming of the victim. This was apart from the act of sacrifice properly so called which consisted in the oblation and the immolation. The ritual closed with the dividing of the flesh according to detailed instructions, first for the priest and his sons and then for the people. The consuming was an integral part of the old sacrificial worship."

[67]Luke 22:42.

the victim). Lastly, He uttered the words, "Consummatum est,"[68] as an indication that everything He needed to undertake for the sake of our healing and salvation was accomplished. His sacrifice was perfect and complete.

These three elements are also present in our own daily sacrifices, if they are a sacrifice in the proper sense. In the past, Catholics would often tell those who were suffering to "offer it up." Modernists during the 1960s through the 1980s ridiculed this as being insensitive and unhelpful. Yet, like all heresy, it was short sighted. This was the phrase said to people so that they could take advantage of their suffering and merit a higher place in heaven by sacrificing their will to God by voluntarily accepting the suffering that He had sent for their purification or for the merit to benefit others. Hence, when a person suffers or denies some good thing, such as through fasting, self denial and the like, he must first make an offering of it to God. If he does not, then it is just a form of dieting, as in the case of fasting, or just bearing it in relation to suffering, etc. In other words, it does not transform the action into a supernatural act of sacrifice by which we offer something to God. We have to die to ourselves and this comes in the form of letting go of some good thing or being willing to suffer what God asks of us. Hence, the slaying of the victim. Lastly, for the sacrifice to be truly meritorious to the degree that it is able, we must be willing to die *completely* to ourselves in relation to the good thing or suffering. In this, our sacrifice is consummated.

Hence, in the context of the sacrifice of the Mass, it is not within the authority of the pope to promulgate a ritual of the Mass without a proper offertory, or by lacking one entirely. This follows from two reasons. The first is the sheer logic of the nature of sacrifice. If he were to promulgate a Mass without a proper offertory or one that lacked an offertory all together, it would not be a proper sacrifice to God, since the Offertory is what distinguishes the action of a

---

[68]John 19:30.

sacrifice from a meal. It would be a contradiction in terms, insofar as he would promulgate something which did not have an essential element of sacrifice, which by its very nature is given to God alone,[69] and yet he would be calling it the Mass, which in the entire tradition of the Church was known to be a sacrifice.

The second is that it is contrary to the Divine Positive Law. When Christ said, "do *this* in commemoration of me," He was specifically commanding the Apostles and their successors to offer the Mass in the manner in which He had done, which included an Offertory,[70] a slaying of the victim ("This is My Body," etc.) and the consummation. Hence, it is not within the authority of the Church or pope to remove or promulgate a liturgy in which these three essential elements of ritualistic sacrifice are lacking.

As to the Consecration, *i.e.*, the slaying of the victim, Gihr observes that: "the essence of the Eucharistic Sacrifice depends neither wholly nor in part on the Communion of the celebrant, but rests solely and entirely in the consecration."[71] He also observes that:

> Not every gift offered to God is a sacrifice. It greatly depends on the manner of offering. Some change or destruction of the gift must take place to constitute a sacrifice. An entire destruction of the gift, or such as is at least morally equivalent, pertains essentially to the idea of sacrifice; hence it must have an outward form. What-ever has not been liturgically transformed (e.g, destroyed), cannot be a real sacrifice (*sacrificium*), but is only a religious gift (*oblatio*), essentially different from sacrifice. Thus we find in all sacrifices

---

[69]ST II-II, q. 85, a. 2.

[70]Luke 22:19. The fact that he gave thanks to God and broke it was an indication of the Offertory. See also 1 Corinthians 11:24.

[71]Gihr, *The Holy Sacrifice of the Mass*, p. 128.

> mentioned in Holy Writ, that there was always some mode of destruction or dissolution appropriate to the nature of the matter of the sacrifice. Thus the animals were slain and their blood poured on the altar, incense was consumed by fire, and wine was poured out. ...The intrinsic and more weighty reason why such a transformation, or destruction, of the gift is requisite for the act of sacrifice lies in the peculiar meaning and in the special object of sacrifice.[72]

The slaying of the victim is seen as an essential element of sacrifice. In the context of the Mass, the slaying of the victim occurs sacramentally by which the Body and Blood of Our Lord are sacramentally split in the dual consecration.[73] This is why Gihr observes that:

> the Eucharistic sacrificial action (*actio sacrificia*) consists in the double consecration, by which the Body and Blood of Christ, under the appearances of bread and wine, are placed in the state of sacrifice and are, therefore, sacrificed. – All the prayers, ceremonies and actions that partly proceed and partly follow the consecration in the celebration of the Mass are, consequently, not essential to the Eucharistic Sacrifice. – The oblation-prayers at the Offertory and after the Elevation, the fraction of the consecrated Host and the co-mingling of a particle of it with the Sacred Blood, are important and profoundly significant constituent parts of the ancient, venerable rite prescribed for the Sacrifice by the Church, but in no wise are they the integral or essential portions of the sacrificial action instituted by Christ. That the Communion of the faithful who are present is not necessary for the Sacrifice, is admitted by all Catholics. – But the case is quite different

---

[72]Ibid., p. 16f.

[73]ST III, q. 78, a. 6.

> with regard to the Communion of the officiating priest. The officiating priest must necessarily communicate at the celebration of the Eucharistic Sacrifice, not merely by reason of a command of the Church, but in virtue of a divine ordinance from Christ Himself. The Communion of the celebrant, therefore, is so necessary, because although it does not appertain to the essence, it is, however, indispensable to the external completeness of the Eucharistic sacrifice; for by this Communion the Sacrifice obtains its end as a food-offering and, consequently, by it the Sacrifice is in a certain sense perfected and consummated. The celebrating priest must partake of the same sacrificial matter which he has just consecrated, in order that the unity of the visible Sacrifice may in its essence and integrity be perfectly secure.[74]

From Gihr's observation, we must make a distinction, therefore, which touches upon the discussion of the quote from the Council of Trent regarding the substance.

In a prior work,[75] this author discussed how the distinctions within the different kinds of value of the Mass are first founded on a distinction between intrinsic and extrinsic value. *The Catholic Encyclopedia* says:

> We must also sharply distinguish between the intrinsic and the extrinsic value of the Mass (*valor intrinsecus, extrinsecus*). As for its intrinsic value, it seems beyond doubt that, in view of the infinite worth of Christ as the Victim and High Priest in one Person, the sacrifice must be regarded as of infinite value, just as the sacrifice of the Last Supper and that of the Cross. But when we turn to the Mass as a sacrifice of impetration and

---

[74]Gihr, *The Holy Sacrifice of the Mass*, p. 199f.

[75]Ripperger, *Topics on Tradition*, p. 113-115.

> expiation, the case is different. While we must always regard its intrinsic value as infinite, since it is the sacrifice of the God-Man Himself, its extrinsic value must necessarily be finite in consequence of the limitations of man. The scope of the so-called "fruits of the Mass" is limited.[76]

The intrinsic value of any valid Mass is infinite since Christ, Who is infinite, is the One Who is offered. Hence, in this respect, every Mass has an infinite value.[77] The Mass, because it is the offering of God the Son to God the Father, gives infinite glory to God.[78]

However, the extrinsic value of the Mass is finite.[79] This is due to the fact that man, a finite creature, is incapable of receiving infinite effects. In this respect, the value of the Mass is "intensive limited,"[80] which means that the fruit of the Mass is limited in its measure. Normally, the liturgical writers state that, as to its impetratory and expiatory value, the Mass is finite,[81] "since the operations of propitiation and impetration refer to human beings, who as creatures can receive a finite act only."[82] When one considers the actual sacrifice of the Mass, which is the sacrifice of Calvary, it is infinite, but as to its

---

[76]OCE, vol. 10, p. 17.

[77]See also, Ludwig Ott, *Fundamentals of Catholic Dogma*, p. 414 and St. Alphonsus Ligouri, *Theologia Moralis*, lib. VI, tract. 3, c. 3, d. 1.

[78]OCE, vol. 10, p. 17.

[79]See also Ott, *Fundamentals of Catholic Dogma*, p. 414.

[80]Gihr, *The Holy Sacrifice of the Mass: Dogmatically, Liturgically and Ascetically Explained*, p. 141.

[81]See OCE, vol. 10, p. 17; Ott, *Fundamentals of Catholic Dogma*, p. 414 and St. Alphonsus Ligouri, *Theologia Moralis*, lib. VI, tract. 3, c. 3, d. 1.

[82]Ott., loc. cit.

effects, it is finite.

Hence, the dual Consecration results in any valid Mass participating in the Calvary sacrifice and, in this sense, the Consecration alone suffices for the sacramental sacrifice. However, the ritual of the Mass around the Consecration is what Christ also commanded by Divine Positive Law and it contains an Offertory, the Consecration, and a Communion. Hence, the substance of the Mass is distinct from the Consecration, while including it. For this reason, there is a distinction between the intrinsic sacrifice (the Consecration) and the extrinsic or ritual sacrifice. The intrinsic sacrifice pertains to the actual Eucharistic or sacramental sacrifice in which Christ becomes present; this is distinct from the ritual sacrifice, which includes all the various elements of the liturgy aside from those things that pertain to the actual Eucharistic or sacramental sacrifice. It is because of this distinction that one must read Gihr's observation that the Offertory and Commuion are unnecessary as only pertaining to the sacramental sacrifice and not the ritual sacrifice.

Yet, a close reading of Gihr in another place yields certain aspects that are, in fact, proper to or essential for a sacrifice. He too makes the distinction between Eucharistic sacrifice and the ritual sacrifice.

> But the case is quite different with regard to the Communion of the officiating priest. The officiating priest must communicate at the celebration of the Eucharistic sacrifice, not merely by reason of a command of the Church, but in virtue of a divine ordinance from Christ Himself. The Communion of the celebrant, therefore, is so necessary because, although it does not appertain to the essence, it is indispensable to the external completeness of the Eucharistic sacrifice; for by this Communion the sacrifice attains its end as a food offering and consequently by it the sacrifice is in a certain sense perfected and consummated! The celebrating priest must partake of the same sacrificial matter which he has

> just consecrated, that the unity of the visible sacrifice may in its essence and integrity be perfectly secured.[83]

Here, Gihr is noting that the Communion of the priest pertains to the essence (of the extrinsic or ritual sacrifice) and is necessary to complete the Eucharistic sacrifice (intrinsic sacrifice). He also observes that this is by the divine ordinance of Christ Himself. While the Offertory and Communion of the priest are not necessary for the actual validity of the Consecration, nevertheless, one cannot have a proper ritual sacrifice without an offertory or a Communion, as is seen in the Old Testament and New Testament. This being said, it would not be within the authority of the pope, not just to promulgate a rite of the Mass that lacked the proper words of Consecration, but also to promulgate a rite which lacked a proper Offertory or a Communion of the priest, due to the commandment of Christ to "do this in commemoration of me." So a proper interpretation of the Council of Trent is rendered in relation to the "substance of the sacraments," regarding the sacrifice of the Mass; it must include the substance of the ritual of the Mass itself.

It is for this reason that we see Cardinal Ratzinger putting forth the following observation:

> The author [Alcuin Reid] expressly warns us against the wrong path up which we might be led by a Neo-scholastic sacramental theology that is disconnected from the living form of the Liturgy. On that basis, people might reduce the "substance" to the matter and form of the sacrament and say: Bread and wine are the matter of the sacrament; the words of institution are its form. Only these two things are really necessary; everything else is changeable. ...Many priests today, unfortunately, act in accordance with this motto. ...They want

---

[83]Gihr, *The Holy Sacrifice of the Mass*, p. 128.

> to overcome the limits of the rite, as being something fixed and immovable, and construct the products of their fantasy, which are supposedly "pastoral", around this remnant, this core that has been spared and that is thus either relegated to the realm of magic or loses any meaning whatever. The Liturgical Movement had in fact been attempting to overcome this reductionism ...and to teach us to understand the Liturgy as a living network of Tradition that had taken concrete form, that cannot be torn apart into little pieces but that has to be seen and experienced as a concrete whole. Anyone who, like me, was moved by this perception at the time of the Liturgical Movement on the eve of the Second Vatican Council can only stand, deeply sorrowing, before the ruins of the very things they were concerned for.[84]

Hence, when the Council of Trent says that the Church, and therefore, the pope can make changes to the liturgy, save the substance of the sacraments, a proper interpretation of that passage in relation to the Mass would not be referring just to the matter and form, but also the substance of the ritual.

Yet, another distinction is necessary. Here, substance of the ritual refers to the fact that any Mass to be in conformity with the Divine Positive Law must include an Offertory, Consecration, and a Communion; the *contents* of those rites could be altered by the pope, provided that it observes all of the other conditions or limitations of his authority.[85] This is why even though most authors agreed that

---

[84]Ratzinger, in Reid, *The Organic Development of the Liturgy,* p. 11.

[85]The insertion of the St. Joseph clause in the canon of the Mass would be an example of this. When it happened in 1962, it did raise some eyebrows, so to speak. Up until that time it was generally considered that the Canon of the Mass, which had been unchanged for 1362 years from the time of St. Gregory the Great was "untouchable" due to the principle of longevity. While most would

some of the parts of the Canon of the Mass are in part from ecclesiastical sources and not necessarily divine or divino-apostolic in origin, nevertheless, the longevity of those elements as well as in many instances of elements which are shrouded in history results in us not being certain as to their source, and this also would limit the papal authority. In other words, since there are parts of the liturgy that we are not certain about, then prudence dictates that they be left alone, especially if they can be shown to be ancient.

Conclusion

In light of the foregoing discussion, a few basic conclusions can be derived regarding the limits of the papal authority. First, it was noted that the pope does have authority over the liturgy, but that authority is limited in various ways and so the following conclusions would necessarily follow:

1) There are certain liturgical elements over which the pope does not have right of determination, insofar as he does not have the right to make changes to them and determine what that element in the liturgy will contain. This would include things such as the essential words of Consecration. In this regard, he does have authority over the element, not as to determination, but as to right of preservation. In other words, even though he does not have a right over what constitutes the matter and form of a valid Eucharist Consecration, he does have the right, *i.e.*, the authority, to enforce by way of ecclesiastical law that all rites of the Church will contain those

---

agree that the insertion poses no theological difficulty as to St. Joseph being mentioned there, there is some debate as to its prudence. Some assert by way of informal discussions that the insertion was a signaling that the Canon was no longer off limits to change, and therefore, problematic, while others assert that this is within the authority of the pope to do so, as to the usefulness of the change for the devotion of the faithful.

essential words. He has an obligation, and therefore authority, to protect the substance of the sacraments against invalidity in the official promulgations of the Church. He would also have a right to enforce in the offering of the Mass that all priests adhere to this prescription, and he has the authority to proscribe any action that is contrary to it. He would also have authority to sanction any priest or bishop who would act contrary to those things over which he does not have a right of determination. In effect, he has authority or right of protection/preservation, but not a right of determination.

2) There are certain elements of the liturgy, *i.e.*, the substance of the sacrifice (ritual), in which the element is such that he does not have the authority over determination as to the existence of the element in the liturgy, but he may have authority or right of determination as to certain aspects of content of that element, but not other elements. This kind of element of the liturgy would include things such as the rite of Communion of the priest or the Offertory. The pope does not have the authority to promulgate a rite without an Offertory, but the pope would have a right to make minor changes to wording or additions of prayers of the Offertory, provided they are within the confines of the various limitations imposed by Divine Positive Law, Natural Law, Apostolicity, longevity, prudence, etc. As to the parts of the elements that are under restriction, due to the limitations of the papal authority over those parts, the pope, again, would have the right and duty of preservation, but not the right of determination. In relation to those elements of the liturgy over which he does not have authority in relation to right of determination, he still has authority over those parts as to right of preservation, insofar as he is the custodian of the elements of sanctification entrusted by Our Lord to the Church.

3) The last kind of liturgical element would be those over which he has a right of determination and preservation, *i.e.*, the *accidentalia,* as they are called. This would include those elements

that do not have any Apostolicity or determination by the Divine Positive Law or Natural Law. As to those elements that have longevity, but which do not fall under originating from the Apostles, the Divine Positive Law or the Natural Law, the restriction in this case has to do with observing the Will of God based upon the longevity. However, it may be possible to make changes in relation to certain aspects of these elements, provided it meets the requirements of supernatural prudence. Prudence would dictate when and if the changes should be made, based upon necessity, authentic Catholic principle, and the good of the faithful; and the pope is free or even in some cases obligated to do so. This would include minor changes to the wording of certain prayers, such as the Collects, Post Communions, Mass compositions for newly canonized saints, the choice of which saints would be commemorated at the altar, and the like. While prudence will show these changes should be done slowly and gradually, the pope does have latitude to do so, as long as it meets the requirements of prudence and the content is not contrary to the Divine Positive Law, Natural Law, Apostolicity, or manifest longevity. This, along with supernatural prudence, will limit innovation, novelty, and error as well as inquietude among the faithful due to the changes, as will be discussed in the chapter on prudence.

Chapter IV: Divino-Apostolic and Apostolic Tradition

Three recurring themes that arise in the context of the discussion of the liturgy from the very beginning, *i.e.*, from the time of the early Fathers until the last century, are matters that pertain to the divine tradition, divino-Apostolic tradition, and Apostolic tradition. References to these three often include either a general observation about certain aspects of the liturgy, which have these as their source and/or which contain a specific element of the liturgy coming directly from Our Lord Himself, from Our Lord to the Apostles, and then to the rest of the Church, or from the Apostles themselves. Sometimes these elements are not clear as to exactly what was passed on (*traditus*). However, sometimes the element, along with the content, is evident in the Deposit of Faith or referenced by one or more Fathers. Obviously, those elements that are in Scripture, or clearly to be known in the Sacred Tradition of the Church, would have the highest certitude. The elements referenced by the Fathers as coming from these three sources would have different degrees of certitude, *i.e.*, everything from little certitude to a commonly held understanding by various Fathers, doctors of the Church and saints throughout history. This varying degree of certitude would envision the fact that some statement made by a particular Father, but not reiterated by others, would normally be given the benefit of the doubt,[1] despite its lack of certitude, especially if no other Father or saint contradicts or questions the assertion about the liturgical element. Others will have a fairly high degree of certitude, as it would be commonly held among the Fathers. To contradict or dismiss these would require proportionate evidence in the tradition itself and not just merely the questioning of modern scepticism.

I. Divine Tradition

To set the scope of the discussion on divine tradition in regard

---

[1]See below on tradition having favor.

to the liturgy, a previously seen quote from Pope Pius XII is quite clear:

> The sacred liturgy does, in fact, include divine as well as human elements. The former, instituted as they have been by God, cannot be changed in any way by men. But the human components admit of various modifications, as the needs of the age, circumstance and the good of souls may require, and as the ecclesiastical hierarchy, under guidance of the Holy Spirit, may have authorized. This will explain the marvelous variety of Eastern and Western rites. Here is the reason for the gradual addition, through successive development, of particular religious customs and practices of piety only faintly discernible in earlier times.[2]

Pius XII distinguishes between those things which come from God and those which come from man, and the human element varies to some degree in an organic development. The thing of importance at this point is to recognize that those things instituted by God cannot be changed, *i.e.*, if Jesus Christ instituted something either Himself (divine tradition) or by commanding and instructing the Apostles (divine-apostolic tradition), then that element is not subject to

---

[2]Pius XII, *Mediator Dei*, para. 50: "Sacra enim Liturgia ut humanis, ita divinis constat elementis; haec autem, ut patet, cum a Divino Redemptore constituta, fuerint, nullo modo ab hominibus mutari possunt; illa vero, prout temporum, rerum animorumque necessitates postulant, varias commutationes habere possunt, quas Ecclesiastica Hierarchia, S. Spiritus auxilio innixa, comprobaverit. Inde miranda illa oritur orientalium atque occidentalium rituum varietas; inde progrediens incrementum proficiscitur, quo peculiares excolendae religionis consuetudines ac peculiaria pietatis opera pedetemptim evolvuntur, et quorum tenue dumtaxat indicium superioribus aetatis habebatur."

change.[3] By way of conclusion, this would mean that the authority of the pope over those elements is that of preservation and not determination, because the content of the element was determined by Our Lord or the Apostles. This was seen in the prior chapter regarding the words of Consecration; the pope does not have the authority over the essential words of Consecration, as they were established by the Lord Himself and are clearly present in Scripture. Also, Our Lord established that the rite of the Mass would have the three elements of the Offertory, Consecration, and Communion by the manner in which

---

[3]Cf. Franzelin, *Tractatus de Sacramentis*, p. 187: "Quando ergo docet Concilium, 'sacramenta novae legis fuisse omnia *a Iesu Christo Domino nostro* instituta,' obvio verborum sensus definitio intelligitur de Iesu Christo institutore visibilis in terris. Etenim documenta et instituta tradita Ecclesiae ab Apostolis post ascensionem Domini, sive in hoc modo Apostoli instuebant multas sacras observationes, caeremonias et ritus etiam ad quam videtur affirmasse, eos habuisse potestatem hoc modo sacramenta instituenda. Hinc distinguit Concilium Tridentinum substantiam sacramentorum, ad cuius mutationem nulla est Ecclesiae potestas, et ritus accedentes ad substantiam, qui subsunt Ecclesiae dispositioni sess. XXI. cap. 2. Posset c) concipi institutio per Apostolos ita, ut post Christi ascensionem Spiritus Sanctus per Apostolos tamquam sua organa revelationis et divinae operationis instituerit aliqua sacramenta." (When, therefore, the Council teaches that "the sacraments of the new law were all instituted by Jesus Christ our Lord," the obvious definition of the meaning of the words is meant of Jesus Christ, the visible institutor on earth. In fact, the documents and institutions handed down by the Church from the Apostles after the Ascension of the Lord, whether in this way the Apostles instituted many sacred observances, ceremonies and rites also seem to affirm that they had the power to institute the sacraments in this way. From this the Council of Trent distinguishes the substance of the sacraments, to change which the Church has no power, and the rites approaching the substance, which are subject to the disposition of the Church. XXI chap. 2. It could be that the institution through the Apostles was conceived in this way, that after Christ's ascension, the Holy Spirit through the Apostles as his organs of revelation and divine work instituted certain sacraments.) See also, ibid., p. 187. It is not in the scope of this book to discuss whether Christ immediately or mediately instituted which sacraments, but whether He or the Apostles commanded certain things to be in the liturgy.

He offered the first Mass and His command to "do *this* in commemoration of me."

However, these two examples provide examples of the distinction mentioned above. There are certain elements of the liturgy that Christ commanded must be in the liturgy and He provided the specific content, *i.e.*, the words of Consecration, or one may say, the actual form of this Sacrament.[4]

Yet, there are other elements that He commanded that had specific content, but which the Apostles evidently understood could be amplified, and here we are thinking of the Offertory.[5] Obviously, the various Offertories, even in the earliest extant texts, are amplified beyond what Our Lord included. These kinds of elements where the content is amplified would seem to be of two kinds, *viz.*, those which include the original content, but then more is added, and those which do not necessarily contain the original content, but the element would still fulfill the prescription of Our Lord regarding that element. In regard to those elements where the content is determined by Our Lord, the pope would not have the authority in regard to

---

[4]The question of the *Mysterium Fidei* will be discussed in a subsequent chapter.

[5]Council of Trent, sess. 22, chpt. IV: "Et cum sancte administrari conveniat sit que hoc omnium sanctissimum sacrificium: ecclesia catholica ut digne reverenter que offerretur ac perciperetur sacrum canonem multis ante saeculis instituit ita ab omni errore purum ut nihil in eo contineatur quod non maxime sanctitatem ac pietatem quandam redoleat mentes que offerentium in deum erigat. Is enim constat cum ex ipsis domini verbis tum ex apostolorum traditionibus ac sanctorum quoque pontificum piis institutionibus." ("And since it is becoming that holy things be administered in a holy manner, and of all things this sacrifice is the most holy, the Catholic Church, to the end that it might be worthily and reverently offered and received, instituted many centuries ago the holy canon, which is so free from error that it contains nothing that does not in the highest degree savor of a certain holiness and piety and raise up to God the minds of those who offer. For it consists partly of the very words of the Lord, partly of the traditions of the Apostles, and also of pious regulations of holy pontiffs.")

determination, but only preservation. In regard to those elements in which the content is not determined by Our Lord, then the pope would have authority to make changes, provided his authority is not restricted in some other way, *e.g.*, by prudence, longevity, etc., as was concluded above.

These distinctions and observations are also seen in the Didache:

> Since, therefore, these things are clear to us, and we have looked into the depths of the divine knowledge, we ought to do in proper order all things which the Master has commanded us to perform at appointed times. He has come out of the offerings and services to be celebrated, and not carelessly nor in disorder, but at fixed times and hours. He has, moreover, by His supreme will, determined where and by whom He wants them to be carried out, so that all may be done in a holy matter, according to His good pleasure and acceptable to His will. Those, then, who make their offerings at the appointed times, are acceptable and blessed; for they follow the laws of the Master and do not sin. To the high priest, indeed, proper ministrations are allotted, to the priest a proper place is appointed, and upon the Levites their proper services are imposed. The layman is bound to the ordinances for the laity.[6]

From the time of the early Church, it was understood that there are distinctions that are made regarding the various liturgical elements. Some of them come directly from Our Lord, and therefore, man may not change them and, as the Didache observes, God Himself did this to ensure that our worship of Him would be rightly ordered.

---

[6]Jurgens, *Faith of the Early Fathers*, p. 10.

II. Apostolic Tradition

A. The Quality of Apostolicity

The importance of Apostolic tradition in connection to the liturgy is already seen to be of importance by virtue of the fact that even what we know is from divine tradition comes via the Apostles. Divino-Apostolic tradition would consist in something being commanded by Our Lord to the Apostles, and they subsequently handed it on to us. This would be distinct from Apostolic tradition, which is something which was inaugurated by the Apostles themselves. If it comes directly from Christ to the Apostles, or from the Holy Spirit to the Apostles, then it is of divine decree and is not subject to the authority of the pope regarding determination. In the case of divino-Apostolic tradition regarding an element of the liturgy, the pope would only have right of preservation, *i.e.*, to protect that specific element in the liturgy.

Yet, when it comes to Apostolic tradition of certain liturgical elements, there is a specific understanding that was enjoyed throughout the history of the Church regarding how those elements were to be approached. Some time after the Protestant reformation when the papal authority over the liturgy was questioned, a particular work was written which clearly shows and defends the papal authority over the liturgy and that is Bouix's *De Iure Liturgico*.

> If the priests of the Lord wanted to keep the ecclesiastical institutions intact, as they were handed down by the blessed Apostles, there would be no diversity, no variety in their orders and consecrations. But since each one, not what has been handed down, but what he sees fit, considers this to be held, hence different things seem to be held or celebrated in different places or churches; and it becomes a scandal to the people who, while they do not know the ancient traditions corrupted by human presumption, think that either the churches do not agree with them, or that they are contrary to what has been brought about by the Apostles or apostolic

> men. For who does not know, or does not notice, that what was handed down by Peter, the chief of the Apostles, of the Roman Church, and is still preserved, must be kept by all; and let nothing be carried over or introduced that has no authority, or seems to take an example from elsewhere.[7]

While there can be certain diversity among the rites, there are certain elements of the liturgy which have been handed down by St. Peter, and therefore, must be kept by all. In other words, if something can be shown to be of Apostolic tradition, normally speaking, it must be in the liturgy regardless of rite. What elements came from St. Peter is difficult in many cases to determine. Even which elements of the Roman canon came from St. Peter himself has been an open topic of discussion for some time. However, the principle is what is important to grasp at this time: if it comes from the Apostles, it is to be held and kept by all.

Franzelin, the writer of one of the most authoritative works on Sacred Tradition[8] ever written, states that:

> When, therefore, the Council teaches that "the sacraments of the new law were all instituted by Jesus Christ our Lord," the

---

[7]Bouix, *De Iure Liturgico*, p. 173: "Si instituta ecclesiastica, ut sunt a beatis apostolis tradita, integra vellent servare Domini sacerdotes, nulla diversitas, nulla varietas in Ipsis ordinibus et consecrationibus haberetur. Sed dum unusquisque non quod traditum est, sed quod sibi visum fuerit, hoc aestimat esse tenendum, inde diversa in diversis locis vel ecclesiis aut teneri aut celebrari videntur; ac fit scandalum populis, qui dum nesciunt traditiones antiquas humana praesumptione corruptas, putent sibi aut ecclesias non convenire aut ab apostolis vel apostolicis viris contrarietatem inductam. Quis enim nesciat aut non advertat, id quod a principe apostolorum Petro Romanae Ecclesiae traditum est, ac nunc usque custoditur, ab omnibus debere servari; nec superduci aut introduci aliquid quod auctoritatem non habeat, aut aliunde accipere videtur exemplum?"

[8]That is, *Tractatus de divina traditione et scriptura.*

> obvious definition of the meaning of the words is meant of Jesus Christ, the visible institutor on earth. In fact, the documents and institutions handed down by the Church from the Apostles after the ascension of the Lord, whether in this way the Apostles instituted many sacred observances, ceremonies and rites also seem to affirm that they had the power to institute the sacraments in this way. From this the Council of Trent distinguishes the substance of the sacraments, to change which the Church has no power, and the rites approaching the substance, which are subject to the disposition of the Church. It could be that the institution through the Apostles was conceived in this way, after Christ's ascension the Holy Spirit through the Apostles as his organs of revelation and divine work instituted certain sacraments.[9]

The reason that what is passed on by the Apostles regarding even the liturgical elements must be kept is because of the fact that if it came from the Apostles, it cannot be assumed that it is just a case of something proceeding from them merely as human beings. Rather, here we begin to see a theme that is repeated from time to time in the tradition, that what the Apostles passed to us in the liturgy contained rites and ceremonies that came from Christ, but also that they were

---

[9]Franzelin, *Tractatus de Sacramentis*, p. 187: "Quando ergo docet Concilium, 'sacramenta novae legis fuisse omnia *a Iesu Christo Domino nostro* instituta,' obvio verborum sensus definitio intelligitur de Iesu Christo institutore visibilis in terris. Etenim documenta et instituta tradita Ecclesiae ab Apostolis post ascensionem Domini, sive in Hoc modo Apostoli instuebant multas sacras observationes, caeremonias et ritus etiam ad quam videtur affirmasse, eos habuisse potestatem hoc modo sacramenta instituenda. Hinc distinguit Concilium Tridentinum substantiam sacramentorum, ad cuius mutationem null est Ecclesiae potestas, et ritus accedentes ad substantiam, qui subsunt Ecclesiae dispositioni sess. XXI. cap. 2. Posset concipi institutio per Apostolos ita, ut post Christi ascensionem Spiritus Sanctus per Apostolos tamquam sua organa revelationis et divinae operationis instituerit aliqua sacramenta."

under the guidance of the Holy Spirit in doing so. The fact that God, both in the Old Testament and New Testament, took pains to make sure our liturgical worship of Him was exact and correct, indicates that when He passed those rites and ceremonies on, and even the authority over the ceremonies in certain respect to the Apostles, He continued to guide them to make sure that what is in the rite of Mass, for example, only contains those things which He wants in the liturgy. It does not mean that further development cannot occur; clearly, it has. Rather, it means that the elements of Apostolic tradition in the liturgy are presumed to be under the guidance of the Holy Spirit, and so historically the Church always treated those elements, to the best of her knowledge, as sacrosanct, *i.e.*, it is the Will of God that they be in the liturgy. Hence, popes would not have thought it within their authority in relation to determination to change or remove such elements, but only to ensure that their preservation remained intact.

Franzelin, reiterates this by observing that:

> all the universal institutions in the Church are distinguished into three orders, so that they are different from the personal ordination and institution of Christ, when He founded the visible Church on earth; another from the ordination of the Apostles according to the authority received from Christ; another, from the law of the Church, the authority of subsequent ages likewise delegated by Christ. Whenever, therefore, Christ is mentioned as the founder of visible institutions and rites in the Church, it is understood that Christ was the visible founder, while He founded the Church on earth and completed the work of redemption. They were the mere promoters of the divine law received by divine revelation and ordination; whether they themselves have been legislators by Apostolic power under the direction of the Holy Spirit, they are not attributed to Jesus Christ in terms of humanity, but to the Holy Spirit (with the exception of those in which the man made himself present to Christ, as in Paul's call to the

> apostleship and in most passages of the Apocalypse). Hence, the Doctors of the schools, who admitted the institution of certain sacraments by the Apostles or by the Church, say that it was done by the Holy Spirit through the Apostles.[10]

Again, if something appears to be instituted by the Apostles, it is not to be presumed it is merely the work of men, but was instituted, guided, and fashioned by the Holy Spirit, using the Apostles as instruments to implement His Will regarding those elements of the liturgy.

Therefore, the quality of Apostolicity in regard to a liturgical element restricts the authority the pope would have over it.[11] Since the Divine Positive Law comes from the Apostles, and the commands of Christ are part of the Divine Positive Law, the popes are bound to follow those commands given to the Apostles by Christ that were not meant for the Apostles alone, but for them and their successors. This would include certain elements in the rite of Mass. The rejection by

---

[10]Ibid., p. 189: "omnia universalia instituta in Ecclesia discernuntur in tres ordines, ut alia sint ex personali ordinatione et institutione Christi, cum visibilis in terra fundaret Ecclesiam; alia ex ordinatione Apostolorum secundum potestatem a Christo acceptam; alia ex lege Ecclesiae subsequentium aetatum potestate item a Christ delegata. Quoties igitur institutorum visibilium ac ritum in Ecclesiae nominatur institutor Christi, intelligatur Christus institutor visibilis, dum in terris Ecclesiam fundaret et opus redemptionis compleret. Iis fuerint meri promulgatores legis divinae acceptae per revelationem et ordinationem divinam; sive fuerint ipsi legislatores potestate apostolica sub directione Spiritus Sancti, non tribuuntur Iesu Christo secundum humanitatem spectato sed Spiritui Sancto (exceptis iis, in quibus Christo homo se praesentem sistebat ut in vocatione Pauli ad apostolatum et in plerisque locis apocalypsis). Unde et veteres ill Doctores scholae, qui aliquorum sacramentorum institutionem per Apostolos vel per Ecclesiam admittebant, eam factam esse dicunt a Spiritu Sancto per Apostolos."

[11]See also Paolo Maria Quarto (or Quarti), *Rubricae Missalis Romani commentariis illustratae, quaest. Fund.*, sec. I, punct. II and punct. IV regarding the importance of Apostolicity.

the pope of the liturgical observances that have been in place throughout the tradition was considered very serious. For example, we read:

> If the pope is able to separate himself without some reasonable cause, but purely by his own will, from the body of the Church and the college of priests through the non-observance of those things which the universal Church observes from the tradition of the Apostles (according to the c. Ecclesi[astic]arum, dist. 11), or because of non-observance of those things which are universally ordained by the ecumenical councils or the authority of the apostolic see, most of all which are ordained for divine worship, such as, by refusing to observe in himself those things which concern the universal state of the Church, or the universal rite of ecclesiastical worship, as if he were to refuse to celebrate in sacred vestments, or in consecrated places, or with candles, or to sign himself with the sign of the cross as does the rest of the college of priests, and similar things, which seem generally ordered to perpetual advantage.[12]

For some authors, if the pope were to not observe the liturgical rites which came from the Apostles, they considered this to be of such import that it would separate him from the body of the Church. Suarez

---

[12]Turcemata, *Summa de ecclesia*, lib. IV, pars Ia, cap. xi, § Secundo sic: "Si papa potest separare se sine aliqua rationabili causa, sed pura voluntate sua a corpore ecclesiae & collegio sacerdotum per non observantiam eorum quae universalis ecclesia ex traditione apostolorum observat: iuxta c. ecclesiarum. dist. 11, aut propter non observantiam eorum quae per universalia concilia, aut apostolicae sedis authoritatem sunt universaliter ordinata, maxime ad cultum divinum, ut puta nolendo observare in se ea quae universalem statum ecclesiae, aut universalem ritum cultus ecclesiastici concernunt, ut quod nollet celebrare in vestibus sacris, aut locis sacratis, aut cum luminaribus, aut signare se signo Crucis sicut residuum sacerdotum collegium facit, & similia, quae ad perpetuam generaliter ordinata videntur utilitatem."

observes:

> ...The Pope could be schismatic, if he did not want to maintain the union and conjunction he should with the whole body of the Church, as if he tried to excommunicate the whole Church, or if he willed to overthrow all ecclesiastical ceremonies established by Apostolic tradition, which Cajetanus noted, 2.2, q. 39.[13]

If the pope would be considered schismatic, if he wanted to overthrow the Apostolic tradition regarding the ceremonies, part of which is the ceremonies of the Mass, this indicates that the quality of Apostolicity on a particular element of the liturgy would render it outside the authority of the pope in regard to determination. In fact, he would be bound to exercise his authority to preserve that element in the liturgy. It is not within the scope of this book to discuss whether the pope would lose his office or even separate himself from the body of the Church by seeking to overthrow the rituals of the Church, since the topic of a heretical pope or a pope who does things that some theologians classify as schismatic would require a rather large volume of its own, considering how much ink has been spilled over that topic in recent years. The point that is germane here is that the theologians considered the quality of Apostolicity of an element of the liturgy to be of the greatest gravity, so much so that it would not be within the authority of the pope to change it. In theory, he could augment it, provided other criteria are met, but to remove it or change it, if it were already specified by the Apostles, is not within his authority.

---

[13]Suarez, *De Caritate*, XII, 1: "Et hoc secundo modo posset Papa esse schismaticus, si nollet tenere cum toto Ecclesiae corpore unionem et conjunctionem quam debet, ut si tentaret totam Ecclesiam excommunicare, aut si vellet omnes ecclesiasticas caeremonias apostolica traditione firmatas evertere, quod notavit Cajetanus, 2.2, q. 39."

B. Certain Elements Enjoy Apostolicity

Yet, there are elements that were specified by the Apostles. This will be discussed more in detail in a subsequent chapter, but it must be demonstrated that the notion that certain elements in the liturgy were specified by the Apostles is shown to be held by those in the tradition. Christ Himself said, "Teaching them to observe all things whatsoever I have commanded you."[14] We also saw above that Christ commanded them to "do *this* in commemoration of me,"[15] which is in the form of a command. However, the obligation of the Apostles to pass on what Christ commanded included not just what we read in Scripture; certain authors in the tradition hold it is more than that. There is implication, even in Scripture, that this could be the case, as we read at the end of the Gospel of John: "But there are also many other things which Jesus did which, if they were written every one, the world itself, I think, would not be able to contain the books that should be written."[16] Gregory IX observes in his work *De Celebratione Missarum* the following:

> If there are any words in the canon which were not spoken by the Evangelists, we must believe that they received them from Christ to the Apostles, and from the Apostles to their

---

[14]Matthew 28:20.

[15]Lk 22:19. cf. 1 Cor 11:24-25. (Emphasis mine.)

[16]John 21:25. There is some speculation that Acts 2:42 could imply there is more. It depends on how the word "prayers" relates to the antecedent of "breaking of the bread": "And they were persevering in the doctrine of the Apostles and in the communication of the breaking of bread and in prayers." ("Erant autem perseverantes in doctrina Apostolorum et communicatione fractionis panis et orationibus.")

> successors."[17]

Pope Gregory is referring to the lineage of liturgical texts and there will be contents of the liturgy which have an Apostolic lineage. Further, what is in the ritual of the Mass, which is from Apostolic lineage, includes matters which are not necessarily included in the Gospels.

To return to a quote above from Franzelin, it was observed that:

> In fact, the documents and institutions handed down by the Church from the Apostles after the ascension of the Lord, whether in this way the Apostles instituted many sacred observances, ceremonies and rites also seem to affirm that they had the power to institute the sacraments in this way. From this the Council of Trent distinguishes the substance of the sacraments, to change which the Church has no power, and the rites approaching the substance, which are subject to the disposition of the Church. (XXI chap. 2). It could be that the institution through the Apostles was conceived in this way, that after Christ's ascension the Holy Spirit through the Apostles as his organs of revelation and divine work instituted certain sacraments.[18]

---

[17]Migne, *Patrologia Latina*, Decretalium D. Gregorii Papae IX, Compilatio titulus XLI, *De Celebratione Missarum, et Sacramento Eucharistiae et Divinis Officiis,*c. VI. (p. 1274): "Si qua verba sunt in canone missae, quae ab Evangelistis dicta non fuerunt, credere debemus, quod a Christo Apostoli, et ab Apostolis eorum successores acceperunt."

[18]Franzelin, *Tractatus de Sacramentis*, p. 187: "Etenim documenta et instituta tradita Ecclesiae ab Apostolis post ascensionem Domini, sive in hoc modo Apostoli instuebant multas sacras observationes, caeromias et ritus etiam ad quam videtur affirmasse, eos habuisse potestatem hoc modo sacramenta instituenda. Hinc distinguit Concilium Tridentinum substantiam sacramentorum, ad cuius

When looking at this passage, not just from the point of view of the quality of Apostolocity being important, but from the point of view of the Apostles actually having passed on sacred observances, ceremonies, and rites, indicates that what the Apostles passed on was more than just what we read in the Gospels, as noted above. This is why St. Thomas says that "the evangelists did not intend to give the forms and rites of the sacraments, but to narrate the words and deeds of Our Lord."[19] What the Apostles passed on, however, was more than that as part of Sacred Tradition. The argument that Christ gave very little instruction to the Apostles or that the Apostles did not convey a ritual any more than what is contained in the Gospels would not be sustainable in light of the general view of the Fathers and statements of the popes. Rather, there was a ritual conveyed by St. Peter, as well as some of the other Apostles,[20] but what was contained in them fully would not be able to be known due to a lack of extant texts. However, this does *not* detract from what is known as conveyed specifically as to certain content of the elements of the rituals by the Patristics, as well as discussed by the saints and popes.

However, there does emerge another criteria by which we know, other than what the Patristics say specifically. This criteria is observed by the author Kenrick, who observes that: "The substance

---

mutationem nulla est Ecclesiae potestas, et ritus accedentes ad substantiam, qui subsunt Ecclesiae dispositioni sess. XXI. cap. 2. Posset concipi institutio per Apostolos ita, ut post Christi ascensionem Spiritus Sanctus per Apostolos tamquam sua organa revelationis et divinae operationis instituerit aliqua sacramenta."

[19]IV Sent., d. 8, q. 2, a. 2a, ad 1: "Evangelistae enim non intendebant formas et ritus sacramentorum tradere, sed dicta et facta Domini enarrare."

[20]Hence, the source of some of the other rites, such as those inaugurated by other Apostles, such as the Chaldean rite by St. Thomas, for example.

of the liturgy, which is the same everywhere, is rightly considered to have flowed from an Apostolic source."[21] This principle would stand to reason, insofar as the Apostles would receive the common teaching from Christ Himself about what is and what is not to be in the liturgy, as was discussed above. When they wrote their respective rites, these rites would incorporate the elements and contents which Christ had determined (or in a certain sense decreed). Modernist arguments that the rites of the Mass in the early Church were no more than what is in the Scriptures, are not sustainable from the point of view of the tradition. Skepticism which is at the root of modernism and its immanentist principle does not suffice to setting aside the tradition on the matter, nor the principles that reason itself would see in the context of liturgical inauguration of rites as well as their development. If a liturgical element and/or its content is consistently in the liturgy of all rites, and is clear throughout time from the beginning, that element is to be presumed to be from Apostolic tradition. Therefore, that element cannot be changed, and the pope would not have authority in relation to right of determination, but would be required, due to the binding force of tradition, to preserve that element and/or content.[22]

III. Quodlibetal Conclusions

The take away from the foregoing is not something lost even on the conciliar and post conciliar theologians. Cardinal Ratzinger himself observed:

---

[21]Kenrick, *Theologia Dogmatica*, vol. 1, p. 253: "Liturgiae substantia, qua ubique eadem est, ex Apostolico fonte manasse merito censetur."

[22]The fact that later authors on occasions say that the pope could change these kinds of elements when necessity would dictate does not enjoy the common opinion of theologians. When reading the Fathers and the theologians onward, they hold that these elements are unchangeable, or at least should be treated as unchangeable.

> Rites ... are forms of the apostolic Tradition and of its unfolding in the great places of the Tradition.... After the Second Vatican Council, the impression arose that the pope really could do anything in liturgical matters.... The First Vatican Council had in no way defined the pope as an absolute monarch. On the contrary, it presented him as the guarantor of obedience to the revealed Word.... The authority of the pope is not unlimited; it is at the service of Sacred Tradition.[23]

This quote actually contains much of what this chapter has said. The papal authority over the liturgy is limited by certain things, such as the divine and Apostolic tradition. The pope is bound by these limitations, since they come from "the revealed Word," which is part of the Divine Positive Law and the fact that the pope is bound by the Sacred Tradition. What then Cardinal Ratzinger was pointing out is what this chapter has seen, which is that the pope being bound by the tradition is something that has been understood and seen throughout the history of the Church. The real issue at the root of all of this is the binding force of the tradition and the acceptance of that reality.[24]

Any rudimentary reading into the monuments of tradition reveals that there are certain elements of the liturgy in which their source is clearly known and others which are not clearly known.

> It is important to note here that, when it comes to the oldest elements of liturgical rites, we often have no way of knowing and may never have the ability to know which of these are of

---

[23] As quoted in Kwasniewski, *From Benedict's Peace to Francis' War*, p. 31.

[24] This is why this author wrote the book *The Binding Force of Tradition*. It was to show that even the pope is bound to the tradition as a remote rule of faith in various ways, and therefore, the principles that govern the liturgy and some of its elements, in varying degrees.

> merely ecclesiastical institution and which are of divine, apostolic, or subapostolic institution, which makes it all the more crucial not to eliminate any of them.[25]

In the subsequent chapter, a specific principle will be seen to apply here, however, at this point, it is important to observe that there should be a certain hesitation on the side of the Church to make changes, when the liturgical source is unknown. It should not be assumed that, because it is unknown, therefore, it can be changed.

Yet, a particular principle comes into view at this stage. Some theologians after the second Vatican Council (not necessarily as a cause of the council) essentially suggested (or at least proceeded) that, if the source was unknown, *i.e.*, there is doubt about the source, then the doubt allowed for the change. Often the particular part of the liturgical element or element itself was considered as dubious simply because it was obscured by the tradition, and so modern man's "superior" judgment in the case was such that it could be followed over the long standing tradition. However, this violates a general principle regarding the tradition, which modernists have at least in practice rejected. Whenever scepticism rules, the scepticism or the questioning was sufficient to throw that aspect of the tradition out and simply ignore it as apocryphal or dubious, and therefore, it can be ignored. This led in some cases to doubting anything unpleasant or that did not fit into the modern mindset.

However, over the course of time, the tradition was vindicated repeatedly, contrary to the modern scepticism. A clear example was the denial and mockery often given to the idea of Our Lady's perpetual virginity by the modernists, who argued that no woman at the time of Our Lady would have ever taken a vow of chastity, since she would want to be the mother of the Messiah. They also asserted the vows of virginity and chastity were a post-Apostolic invention and

---

[25]Kwasniewski, *True Obedience*, p. 85, ft. 41.

were not present at the time of Christ. Then came the Qumran findings, some of which dated to the time of or just before the time of Christ, which contained references to members of the Essenes taking vows. This is an example of the general principle "when in doubt, favor is on the side of the tradition.[26] This principle safeguards against falling into elementary error, both in regard to matters of the faith, and also in historical matters. It is not until there is positive proof to the contrary that a tradition would be set aside. Yet, even when this occurs, the proof contrary to a putative tradition must itself come from the tradition, *i.e.*, the monuments. Lack of proof from the monuments themselves always defaults to the putative tradition remaining normative.

This is also true in relation to the liturgy, *i.e.*, favor is on the side of the tradition. When the liturgical discussion happened in the 1940s through the 1960s, the liturgical studies, again, were by and large nascent and did not have the depth that is just now starting to emerge regarding these matters. Hence, as a matter of caution, there should have been a more moderated judgment at that time that the studies needed to mature more before any real suggestions were made about the liturgical changes. Historically, the Church trimmed the tree of the liturgy, but never cut down the trunk, primarily as a matter of Fear of the Lord and basic caution.

Bouix goes on to make the following observation, which can be seen more fully in light of the various aspects of the liturgy discussed in this chapter. We quote it again:

> If the priests of the Lord wanted to keep the ecclesiastical institutions intact, as they were handed down by the blessed Apostles, there would be no diversity, no variety in their orders and consecrations. But since each one, not what has been handed down, but what he sees fit, considers this to be

---

[26]Hence St. Paul's admonition (2 Thes 2:15): "hold fast to the traditions."

> held, hence different things seem to be held or celebrated in different places or churches; and it becomes a scandal to the peoples who, while they do not know the ancient traditions corrupted by human presumption, think that either the churches do not agree with them, or that they are contrary to what has been brought about by the Apostles or apostolic men. For who does not know, or does not notice, that what was handed down by Peter, the chief of the Apostles, of the Roman Church, and is still preserved, must be kept by all; and let nothing be carried over or introduced that has no authority, or seems to take an example from elsewhere.[27]

This quote observes that there can be certain diversity among the rites, but there are certain elements of the liturgy which have been handed down by St. Peter, and therefore, must be kept by all. In other words, if something can be shown to be of Apostolic tradition, normally speaking, it should be kept by all, as was observed. This sets the parameters for any liturgical changes and what should and should not be changed. If it comes from Apostolic tradition, then the subsequent liturgical tradition is bound to that element or part of the element of the liturgy.

To quote again Pius XII, which makes this clear:

---

[27]Bouix, *De Iure Liturgico*, p. 173: "Si instituta ecclesiastica, ut sunt a beatis apostolis tradita, integra vellent servare Domini sacerdotes, nulla diversitas, nulla varietas in Ipsis ordinibus et consecrationibus haberetur. Sed dum unusquisque non quod traditum est, sed quod sibi visum fuerit, hoc aestimat esse tenendum, inde diversa in diversis locis vel ecclesiis aut teneri aut celebrari videntur; ac fit scandalum populis, qui dum nesciunt traditiones antiquas humana praesumptione corruptas, putent sibi aut ecclesias non convenire aut ab apostolis vel apostolicis viris contrarietatem inductam. Quis enim nesciat aut non advertat, id quod a principe apostolorum Petro Romanae Ecclesiae traditum est, ac nunc usque custoditur, ab omnibus debere servari; nec superduci aut introduci aliquid quod auctoritatem non habeat, aut aliunde accipere videtur exemplum."

> The sacred liturgy does, in fact, include divine as well as human elements. The former, instituted as they have been by God, cannot be changed in any way by men. But the human components admit of various modifications, as the needs of the age, circumstance and the good of souls may require, and as the ecclesiastical hierarchy, under guidance of the Holy Spirit, may have authorized. This will explain the marvelous variety of Eastern and Western rites. Here is the reason for the gradual addition, through successive development, of particular religious customs and practices of piety only faintly discernible in earlier times.[28]

Pius XII distinguishes between those things which come from God and those which come from man and the human element varies to some degree in an organic development. The thing of importance at this point is to recognize that those things instituted by God cannot be changed, *i.e.*, if Jesus Christ instituted something either Himself (divine tradition) or by commanding and instructing the Apostles (divine-apostolic) tradition, then that element is not subject to change.[29]

---

[28]Pius XII, *Mediator Dei*, para. 50: "Sacra enim Liturgia ut humanis, ita divinis constat elementis; haec autem, ut patet, cum a Divino Redemptore constituta, fuerint, nullo modo ab hominibus mutari possunt; illa vero, prout temporum, rerum animorumque necessitates postulant, varias commutationes habere possunt, quas Ecclesiastica Hierarchia, S. Spiritus auxilio innixa, comprobaverit."

[29]Cf. Franzelin, *Tractatus de Sacramentis*, p. 187: "Quando ergo docet Concilium, 'sacramenta novae legis fuisse omnia *a Iesu Christo Domino nostro* instituta,' obvio verborum sensus definitio intelligitur de Iesu Christo institutore visibilis in terris. Etenim documenta et instituta tradita Ecclesiae ab Apostolis post ascensionem Domini, sive in Hoc modo Apostoli instuebant multas sacras observationes, caeremonias et ritus etiam ad quam videtur affirmasse, eos habuisse potestatem hoc modo sacramenta instituenda. Hinc distinguit Concilium Tridentinum substantiam sacramentorum, ad cuius mutationem null est Ecclesiae

Even if the element or part of the element as found in the tradition does not have a high theological note, it is still binding unless there is positive proof in the monuments bearing greater theological note to the contrary. This is an important observation and principle, since it contradicts the general modern approach, which says that if the theological note of a particular element of the liturgy is not high, *i.e.*, there is not much support in the tradition, even though a saint here or there might reference it, then it can be set aside. This practice has to be moderated and duly critically examined, since many times something may be referenced here and there by a particular Father of the Church or some saint, but it was not commonly referenced due to the fact that it was generally known by all to be the case. If it is not the case that it was commonly known or accepted, due to the obscurity in the tradition or the general lack of support in the tradition, then the matter defaults to the principle above about the favor being on the side of tradition.

---

potestas, et ritus accedentes ad substantiam, qui subsunt Ecclesiae dispositioni sess. XXI. cap. 2. Posset concipi institutio per Apostolos ita, up post Christi ascensionem Spiritus Sanctus per Apostolos tamquam sua organa revelationis et divinae operationis instituerit aliqua sacramenta." (When, therefore, the Council teaches that "the sacraments of the new law were all instituted by Jesus Christ our Lord," the obvious definition of the meaning of the words is meant of Jesus Christ, the visible institutor on earth. In fact, the documents and institutions handed down by the Church from the Apostles after the Ascension of the Lord, whether in this way the Apostles instituted many sacred observances, ceremonies, and rites also seem to affirm that they had the power to institute the sacraments in this way. From this the Council of Trent distinguishes the substance of the sacraments, to change which the Church has no power, and the rites approaching the substance, which are subject to the disposition of the Church. XXI chap. 2. It could be that the institution through the Apostles was conceived in this way, up after Christ's ascension the Holy Spirit through the Apostles as his organs of revelation and divine work instituted certain sacraments.)" See also, ibid., p. 187. It is not in the scope of this book to discuss whether Christ immediately or mediately instituted which sacraments, but whether He or the Apostles commanded certain things to be in the liturgy.

There is one more final conclusion that can be drawn from the discussion in this chapter. If the pope is bound to retain those elements that are divine or divino-apostolic tradition, then the priest is likewise bound to offer Mass according to a rite that contains those elements or parts of elements. It binds not just the pope, but also the priests and bishops, in order to be true to the command that Christ gave to the Apostles of the various parts, and also the Apostles themselves who inserted those elements into the liturgy. This is the true force behind the document *Quo Primum* of Pope St. Pius V, issued in 1570.[30] Since these elements come from those two sources, no ecclesiastical authority, not even the pope, can forbid a priest from offering Mass which contains liturgical elements which fall into those two categories. To put it more clearly, even though the pope may make certain determinations about which rites may or may not be said, the pope must provide in the determinations a rite which contains these elements. This is what undergirds Pope St. Pius V's asserting that no one can deny the priests the right to offer the rite of Mass which contains those elements which have been faithfully preserved throughout history, particularly referencing the rite which he promulgated. Moreover, the various other aspects discussed in this text support the fact that the Mass, which Pope St. Pius V promulgated, contains the divine as well as divino-Apostolic

---

[30]It is the *opinion* of this author that *Quo Primum* as such does not enjoy *ex cathedra* status in the sense of being infallible. A close reading of the Latin shows that the language is canonical and not doctrinal. Some English translations do not accurately reflect that aspect of the document, and so some have concluded that the document was infallible by nature. It is not the intention of the author to enter into that debate, but to draw attention to the fact that there are some things that are theologically certain that undergird the document. The reason it is binding, even on subsequent popes and generations as to its principles and some of its conclusions, is precisely because it presumes and is based on the understanding of the binding force of the divine and divino-Apostolic aspects of liturgical tradition. Hence, no pope can derogate from those things which bind from those two sources.

traditions, but it also faithfully preserves the additions which were inserted by various saints and popes in an authentic organic liturgical development, those elements cannot be denied the right of use to the priests and bishops of the Church due to that longevity.

Chapter V. Supernatural Prudence as a *Regula* for Liturgical Change

Having discussed briefly the general principles governing liturgical change and the limits of papal authority over the liturgy, it becomes necessary to discuss what the concrete conclusions would be regarding what can and cannot be changed. However, to go from the general principles to concrete action is the domain of the virtue of prudence, which plays a key role when the pope is judging whether changes are necessary, which changes are necessary, and when they should be done. In other words, it is the virtue of prudence which bridges the gap between the general principles and the concrete application of those principles.[1]

I. Prudence in General

St. Thomas defines prudence in two different ways, but the two definitions convey the same meaning, *viz.*, "the application of right reason to action,"[2] and "right reason of action."[3] Prudence is a virtue in the practical intellect as in a subject.[4] Because it resides in reason, prudence perfects reason[5] as to its operations in relation to practical matters.[6] Since prudence deals with actions, *i.e.*, practical

---

[1]The following section on prudence is taken in part from Ripperger, *Introduction to the Science of Mental Health*, vol. III, part II (p. 716-756).

[2]ST II-II, q. 47, a. 4 and 8: "applicatio rectae rationis ad opus."

[3]ST I-II, q. 57, a. 5, De Vir., q. 5, a. 1, ad 3 and In Ethic. VI, l. 7 (n. 1196): "recta ratio agibilium."

[4]ST I-II, q. 56, a. 2, ad 4; ibid., a. 3; ST II-II, q. 47, aa. 2 and 5 and De Vir., q. 1, a. 6.

[5]ST I-II, q. 61, a. 2.

[6]St. Thomas observes in III Sent., d. 33, q. 1, a. 1b that prudence makes right reason.

matters, prudence helps the person to know what is to be done.[7] In relation to the pope and liturgical changes, prudence will direct him in his judgment, along with the aid of grace of office, to know what needs to be changed and what does not, and how the changes should occur, if they are to occur at all.

St. Thomas says that prudence helps one to reason well so that he may live a whole life well.[8] Prudence does not just help the person in a particular case to know what should be done, but it also helps the person to know how a particular action affects his whole life. In this respect, as we will see with foresight, prudence helps to know what would be good, not just to satisfy the desires and wishes of a segment of the Church, but for the whole Church and its continued right worship moving forward into the future.

In relation to actions, there are two things: the end (*finis*) and the means to the end (*ea quae sunt ad finem*). Prudence has a specific kind of relationship to the end and the means. As to the end, prudence orders the means to the end;[9] if it is acquired prudence, it is a natural end; if it is infused prudence, it is a supernatural end. The ends of prudence are pre-established, by being either naturally known or known through science; hence, prudence does not establish the ends.[10] Thus, the ends of human nature are pre-established by human nature[11] or, we may say by, the Natural Law. Man is naturally inclined to specific ends which differ from the ends of cows, bats, and other animals. Hence, man cannot choose his ends because they are

---

[7]ST II-II, q. 47, a. 1, ad 2.

[8]Ibid., q. 47, a. 2, ad 1 and ibid., q. 47, a. 13. In ST I-II, q. 57, a. 5, St. Thomas notes interestingly that prudence helps one to act well and *to be good*.

[9]ST II-II, q. 47, a. 1, ad 2; ibid., q, 47, aa. 2 and 5.

[10]ST II-II, q. 47, a. 6.

[11]III Sent., d. 33, q. 2, a. 3 and ST II-II, q. 47, a. 15.

predetermined by nature, *e.g.*, man is ordered, whether he likes it or not, to the end of marriage. But man can freely intend to order a means to that end or not; in other words, man has the capacity to choose the means which will help him achieve that end.

These ends may be naturally known,[12] *e.g.*, most people know that man is ordered toward marriage, living in common and things of this sort. But some ends are only known through science (philosophy and theology) and by this is meant that only after a formal study of human nature and the Natural Law is someone able to know with certitude whether something is an end or not, for man. In effect, one's conception of man determines one's prudential judgments.[13]

This is why the discussion of how modern man is different from his predecessors can be problematic, when done by certain authors. We know that human nature does not change as essences do not change.[14] We also know that the Deposit of Faith does not change, *i.e.*, revelation or the Divine Positive Law, and therefore, any consideration of prudential changes in the liturgy would take this reality into account. In other words, modern man was NOT different

---

[12]Synderesis is the connatural habit (ST II-II, q. 47, a. 5, ad 3) which establishes the ends which determine prudential reasoning (ibid., ad 1). Synderesis affects the major premise of the practical syllogism, see below.

[13]This will become even more manifest in the discussion of the application of universals to particulars.

[14]The idea that essences do not change started with Plato, continued with Aristotle and was present in the Catholic philoposhical tradition through Aquinas, even to the present age. See OCE, vol. V, p. 543f "Essence is properly described as that whereby a thing is what it is, an equivalent of the τὸ τί ἦν εἶναι of Aristotle (Metaph., VII, 7)." The OCE observes that for Aristotle, the essences are eternal and, therefore, unchanging. This is implied in the very Greek above which is translated as "that which is to be." The very phrase for Aristotle implies something eternal. This is also why the principle regarding definitions is formulated the way it is as well (Weullner, *Summary of Scholastic Principles*, p. 69): "An essential definition is one, constant, immutable, necessary, eternal, and indivisible."

than any of his predecessors as far as his human nature was concerned, as well as the reality of his laboring under the exact same disorders of original and actual sin known through Revelation, and therefore, what his obligations are to enjoy the redemption of Christ known through the Divine Positive Law. The fact that technology had advanced, as well as that philosophy had essentially collapsed (at least from the Thomist point of view), did not change the reality of who man was. These things are purely accidental, and therefore, would not alter substantially how prudence was applied in the modern context.

To continue on the discussion of prudence, since we can choose to direct means to specific ends, prudence helps one to relate by conforming to right ends,[15] *i.e.*, prudence helps one to direct his life to the right ends for his life. Hence, if a person is not prudent, he will not direct his actions or conform himself to the right ends of human nature. This is precisely the problem seen in some discussions of liturgical changes: the liturgical changes proposed often direct the liturgical actions to ends which do not suit human nature, or they use unsuitable means to a good end. For example, certain liturgical changes proposed that the liturgy conform to people's emotions or desires, rather than their true spiritual good. St. Thomas observes that any malice (vicious habit) corrupts right estimation of the end.[16] In effect, those, who have misdirected the means to the wrong ends or even the right ends, do not have a proper understanding of the end. If we translate this more theologically, it signifies that those who do not have virtue or who do not believe the teachings of the Church do not have a right estimation about human nature, which is ordered to specific ends. They also lack a right belief in Who God is and how He is to be approached or treated, *i.e.*, they do not often have Fear of the Lord in the proper sense, and therefore, risk offending Him in their proposed liturgical changes.

---

[15] III Sent., d. 33, q. 1, a. 1b.

[16] In Ethic., VI, l. 4 (n. 1170).

As to the means, St. Thomas has a great deal to say. The means has two components to it, viz., the object or the action and the circumstances surrounding the action. With respect to the action, St. Thomas observes that prudence helps establish the mean (*medium*) with respect to the means (*ea quae sunt ad finem*).[17] Virtue lies in the mean;[18] this indicates that the person does not go to excess or defect in his actions, so that his actions will not exceed or fall short of the end which he is trying to achieve. Prudence helps one to judge whether a given course of action will go to excess or defect in relation to the end, *e.g.*, in order to be physically healthy, prudence helps one to know that eating half a hamburger may not be enough, but that five hamburgers are too many. Therefore, prudence would judge that two hamburgers for a large grown man is a good mean. In the context of the liturgy, supernatural prudence which has God as the end, would know when a specific liturgical change would be suitable to how God is to be addressed, treated, or approached. If a person's judgments are based on the principle of immanence (*i.e.*, he is a modernist), he is likely to judge to excess or defect in relation to the means, which is why his actions cause so much theological and liturgical damage. For this reason, St. Thomas says that prudence helps reason to relate suitably to the means (*ea quae sunt ad finem*).[19] From this, it becomes clear that any modernist or heretic could never be trusted with liturgical discussions or changes.

In relation to the circumstances surrounding the action, the fundamentals of prudence become clearer. Prudence helps one to judge rightly, *i.e.*, to know circumstances which are singulars.[20]

---

[17]III Sent., d. 33, q. 2, a. 3 and II-II, q. 47, a. 7.

[18]See volume one, chapter ten (IV) of Ripperger, *Introduction to the Science of Mental Health*.

[19]ST I-II, q. 57, a. 5.

[20]That prudence helps one to know the singulars, see II-II, q. 47, a. 3.

Circumstances which surround an action take the consideration of the action from an abstract affair to one in which the person must consider concretely how the action relates to the given circumstances. This is why St. Thomas says that even though nature inclines us to some end that is predetermined, the actions in relation to the end are diversified according to persons and affairs,[21] or we may say according to circumstances.

It is here that we come to the discussion of the perception of those members in the Church who were in positions of the Magisterium and academia in the Church during the 1960s. Hindsight is 20/20, as they say, and so today we are in a better position to judge, due to detachment from the events of the 1950s and the 1960s, more objectively the circumstances of the time. In other words, were the circumstances of the 1940s through the 1960s such that it was necessary to make significant liturgical changes?[22] What we have learned is that the 1940s through the 1960s were a time of great moral and spiritual upheaval, even in the Church. These issues did not arise out of a vacuum, but were the result of moral issues already present

---

[21]See ST II-II, q. 47, a. 5.

[22]Here we are reminded of the often observed assertion made about the fathers of Vatican II (Response to the dubia of *Traditiones Custodes*); "One fact is undeniable: The Council Fathers perceived the urgent need for a reform so that the truth of the faith as celebrated might appear ever more in all its beauty, and the People of God might grow in full, active, conscious participation in the liturgical celebration [cf. *Sacrosanctum Concilium* n. 14], which is the present moment in the history of salvation, the memorial of the Lord's Passover, our one and only hope. It should not grant permission to use the Rituale Romanum and the Pontificale Romanum which predate the liturgical reform; these are liturgical books which, like all previous norms, instructions, concessions and customs, have been abrogated." We do not deny that the Council Fathers were convinced that changes needed to be made. What is being questioned here is whether their perceptions of the time in which they lived were accurate or not.

in the seminaries and academia of the 1950s.[23] If anything, since prudence requires a clear grasp of the circumstances, which requires virtue,[24] the 1940s through the 1960s were, in hindsight, one of the least of times to consider changes to the liturgy.[25]

Since prudence helps the person to know the action *to be taken*, prudence deals with future outcomes to specific kinds of actions. Hence, to know the future from knowledge of the present or past pertains to prudence.[26] Since the future is contingent, because the possible outcomes of one's actions can vary, prudence deals with contingents.[27] Prudence helps one to read the circumstances based

---

[23]The very issuance of the document *Religiosorum Institutio* by the Congregation of Religious in 1960 is a clear testimony to this fact, as well as the reality that, one can begin to see the collapse of the Natural Law in the minds of moral theologians during the 1950s, which allowed for certain kinds of mutual acts among the married that were condemned by the Church as well as theologians as against the Natural Law. This was a sign that modern man was not any different from his predecessors in the area of sin and redemption. The fact that arguments about contraception raged during the third session of Vatican II, so much so that Paul VI had to pull it from the floor of discussion, and the later rejection by a significant segment of bishops and theologians of *Humanae Vitae,* is itself a testimony that many of those of the time who were influential in liturgical discussions did not have sufficient virtue to have a clear grasp of "modern man" or the "modern world." These are just a couple of virtually countless examples that could be proffered.

[24]See below.

[25]We recall St. Ignatius' principle that one ought not make changes or decisions in times of consolation (elation) or desolation. The post war desolation and euphoria of the age resulted in a set of circumstances where important changes should have been delayed or simply not made.

[26]ST II-II, q. 47, a. 1.

[27]III Sent., d. 33, q. 2, a. 2a; ST I-II, q. 57, a. 5, ad 3 and ST II-II, q. 49, a. 1. Also, circumstances are contingents because they could be otherwise than they are in a particular case, since God can change history to modify the

upon past experience to see the possible (contingent) outcomes of the course of action.

In the context of the liturgy, this means that any proposed liturgical changes will take into consideration man's unchanging nature and state (at least until Christ returns), and the unchanging Deposit of Faith, and therefore, any proposed change would be perennial. Any changes made would stand the test of time and not be bound to a specific time and culture. The proposed changes made in the 1960s seemed to have locked the Church into a "time warp." In other words, the liturgical changes proposed resulted in the Mass being time bound to the 1960s. We see this in the forms of expression, what is considered important, the reduction of the sacred, etc., which are all hallmarks of the 1960s. This also has led to church designs, liturgical appointments such as chalices, vestments, altars, etc., being very reminiscent today in the 2000s, of the 1960s. But any liturgical change should be able to stand the test of time and in that sense should be timeless. It should have the ability to appeal to every age and every generation. If the loss of the youth after the liturgical changes is any indication and the attraction of the youth to the Mass of the Ages is any further indication, it is a sign that the youth of this generation does not find the liturgies designed in the 1960s to address them today. Whereas, a timeless liturgy will attract men of virtue of every age, every culture, and every generation.

Since prudence requires knowledge of human nature and of circumstances, it requires knowledge of universals and particulars.[28] Prudence applies the universal principles and knowledge known by the possible intellect about man and his ends to the concrete, particular,

---

circumstances in which one finds oneself.

[28]In Ethic., VI, l. 6 (n. 1194). In ST II-II, q. 47, a. 3, St. Thomas notes that prudence knows the universal principles of reason and singulars, about which actions are concerned.

and singular in which he must act.[29] For example, a person may know the universal principle that eating excessively is bad for one's health. But when he is sitting at the dinner table and a large amount of food is placed before him, he must apply the universal principle in the concrete. How hungry is he? How much does his body require so that he does not become weak and ill? Based upon past experience, he then judges how much he should eat so that he does not eat excessively.

This general principle is applied in the concrete by the possible intellect converting back to the phantasm to judge how much he should eat.[30] So that he can properly apply the universal principle, *i.e.*, judge the universal principle's applicability to the phantasm, the phantasm must be properly prepared. For this reason, prudence requires rectitude of appetite about the end for which the person is striving.[31] Obviously, if the concupiscible and irascible appetites suffer from vice, their disordered passions will affect the phantasm and thereby affect prudential judgment. This is why those who have charge of making liturgical changes *must* be men of preeminent virtue, so that their appetites are moderated by virtue and do not affect their judgment about what suits the liturgy.

Yet, one also needs rectitude of the rational appetite, *viz.*, the will.[32] If a person is ill-willed, even if he knows the proper universal principles, he will not apply them concretely, since he does not want to do so. Moreover, he will affect the phantasms by the disorder of his will redounding to the imagination which will affect his prudential judgment. For this reason, the liturgical changes were considered to

---

[29]ST II-II, q. 47, a. 3, ad 1 and ibid., q. 47, a. 6.

[30]The possible intellect must convert back to the phantasm since that is where the singular is known.

[31]In Ethic., VI, l. 4 (n. 1173).

[32]ST I-II, q. 56, a. 2, ad 3 and ibid., q. 56, a. 3.

be "the prerogative of saints." This proceeded from two necessary suppositions. The first is that a saint will likely have true Fear of the Lord and, thereby, avoid introducing into the liturgy anything that would offend God, *i.e.*, he would have sufficient rectitude of appetite not to do his own will in the matter. This also avoids anyone who might have an agenda harmful to the Church from ever having any influence over the liturgy of the Church. The second is that when the liturgy is entrusted to the saints to study and make the changes, they were often erudite men, *i.e.*, they have a great knowledge of Catholic theology, and therefore, know what form of prayer conforms to it. They also know the limitations of their knowledge and will not make changes over something they do not know.[33]

Prudence is perfected not by the exterior senses but by the interior senses, one of which is memory.[34] Through experience of past events, one learns about the possible outcomes of future events. Here we see two essential criteria for prudence; the first is experience, not just any kind of experience, but the right kind of experience. If one is always around others who make wrong decisions and one never learns the proper outcome for which one should strive, he will not have the right experiences by which he can judge properly. Experience is what is stored in memory, so the right memories are necessary for prudence. Since memories are required, young people do not have prudence,[35] as a general rule, because they lack experience (memories)

---

[33]This issue will be revisited later.

[34]ST II-II, q. 47, a. 3, ad 2.

[35]That acquired prudence is not in the young, see ST II-II, q. 47, a. 14, ad 3.

by which to judge what to do. Prudence is normally[36] in the elderly;[37] because of the process of aging, they are more materially disposed toward clearer phantasms and they lack the motions of the passions. The elderly also have more experience, and therefore, more memories from which to draw on. In fact, those who are inexperienced will often be overwhelmed by circumstances, since there can be an infinite number of circumstances and experience is necessary to know which circumstances affect the given course of action and which do not. Through experience, the infinite number of possible singulars are reduced to a finite number, since the person knows what happens in most cases.[38]

When liturgical changes are to be contemplated, only those with sufficient age and memory should be consulted. Here we are not just talking about mere number of years, although that should be part of it. Here we are talking about the Church's memory in the analogical sense. No man who does not have a thorough and deep knowledge of the tradition of the Church, which is the Church's memory, should ever be in a position to suggest changes. Here we are not talking about being an academic, although he may be. Here we are referring to his life-long study of the history and tradition of the Church. He will know, not just how the Church has dealt with these things in the past, he will have a sense of the flow of the history of these things and can see where the Holy Spirit is leading the Church *based on its past*, not just what he wants in the future or here and now.

In order to be prudent, the phantasm has to be properly

---

[36]The presumption here is that the older person has tried to lead a virtuous life. This is not always the case.

[37]ST II-II, q. 47, a. 15, ad 2.

[38]ST II-II, q. 47, a. 3, ad 2.

prepared by the cogitative power.[39] Prudence perfects particular reason (cogitative power) to the right estimation of singular operable intentions.[40] While prudence is in the possible intellect as in a subject, nevertheless as one acts prudently and has rightly ordered experience, the cogitative power is trained to discern which experiences (sense data about singulars) fit the phantasms that are present in the imagination. In this way, the cogitative power prepares the phantasm for a proper prudential judgment. If the cogitative power has bad habits, the phantasms simply will not be prepared properly, and the person will have a hard time applying the universals known in the possible intellect to the concrete circumstances known through the phantasm. In a word, he will not think clearly. This is also why, when people perform the actions of virtue over the course of time, they experience a kind of clarity of mind.

Again, this is why both the timing and men chosen to make any necessary liturgical changes are key. The worst possible time to make liturgical changes is when the Church would be or is going through major shifts in its thinking, the culture is showing clear signs of deviating from Christianity, the society has just come out of traumatic events (such as world wars), etc. All of these experiences will cause a lack of clarity in phantasms among those of that generation, and thereby, affect their judgment about what is suitable in the liturgy. Furthermore, only the saints should make liturgical changes, since even if they have been wounded or have gone through tremendous suffering, they will not have reached the heights of sanctity without first healing. Yet, as a general rule, even among the saints, it is best to consign this task to the most knowledgeable, the most psychologically balanced, well formed men and not those who

---

[39]Many of the statements made in this chapter require a proper understanding of the psychological faculties as understood by St. Thomas in his various works.

[40]In Ethic., VI, l. 9 (n. 1215).

have a name, a reputation, a position in academia, etc.

From all of this one grasps, therefore, that acquired prudence is gained through action.[41] Since prudence directs actions, and since all of the other moral virtues are obtained, increased or decreased through action, prudence is the cause of the other moral virtues.[42] There is a redundancy of prudence to the other virtues,[43] because prudence directs the other virtues.[44] One cannot be temperate, for example, without being prudent. St. Thomas makes the following observation:

> prudence not only directs the moral virtues in choosing those which are to the end [means], but also in determining the end. Moreover, the end of each moral virtue is to attain the mean of its proper matter, which indeed the mean is determined according to the right reason of prudence.[45]

Even though the end of human nature is that, for example, we eat food, prudence must set the amount (*medium aut finis*) of the food so that one does not eat too much or too little (*ea quae sunt ad finem*). It is up to prudence to establish the mean for the other moral virtues and so one cannot have any of the other moral virtues without

---

[41]ST II-II, q. 47, a. 14, ad 3.

[42]De Vir., q. 1, a. 6.

[43]ST I-II, q. 61, a. 4.

[44]Ibid. and III Sent., d. 33, q. 2, a. 5. See also De Vir., q. 1, a. 6.

[45]ST I-II, q. 66, a. 3, ad 3: "Prudentia non solum dirigit virtutes morales in eligendo ea quae sunt ad finem, sed etiam in praestituendo finem. Est autem finis uniuscuiusque virtutis moralis attingere medium in propria materia, quod quidem medium determinatur secundum rectam rationem prudentiae."

prudence.[46] On the other hand, prudence requires the other moral virtues.[47] This follows from our previous discussion where it was mentioned that if the appetites, both intellective and sensitive, lack virtue, their disordered passions and motions (as in the case of the will) will affect the phantasm in the imagination, and thereby, affect the judgment of prudence. Therefore, the more just, fortitudinous, and temperant one is, the more prudent one can be, because he will have clearer phantasms.

Why go into this level of detail about the virtue of prudence in a book on liturgy? Ultimately, it is because, in fact, the very discussion that liturgical changes should be made is based in prudence. Yet, if an age is fraught with lack of temperance,[48] fortitude,[49] and justice,[50] that is a clear indicator that prudence is lacking as well. This is precisely the time when liturgical changes should not be made.

II. The Integral Parts of Prudence

Prudence is a cardinal virtue[51] and can be subdivided into the subjective parts of prudence. Prudence also has potential parts, *i.e.*,

---

[46]St. Thomas says in III Sent., d. 33, q. 2, a. 1c, ad 2 that prudence guides all moral matters.

[47]De Vir., q. 5, a. 2.

[48]The free love movement of the 1960s did not come out of a vacuum; it came from the beatnik culture of the 1950s. See Lachman, *Turn off Your Mind.*

[49]This is based on the fact that many from the greatest generation after fighting in the Second World War openly said they would never do it again.

[50]The fresh memory in people's minds (fewer than 20 years prior) of the horrors of the Second World War was a clear indicator that justice was not alive and well in the past century.

[51]III Sent., d. 33, q. 2, a. 1c; De Vir., q. 1, a. 12, ad 26 and ibid., q. 5, a. 1.

virtues which are annexed to prudence, because of the nature of their matter, but which are not part of prudence *per se*.[52] Yet, prudence has integral parts, *i.e.*, other virtues without which prudence could not exist. To get a better grasp on the practical aspect of how prudence impacts the discussion of the liturgy, it is important to understand the integral parts of prudence and how they affect liturgical theology.

A. Memory (*Memoria*)

The first integral part of prudence is memory. This integral part of prudence is the *virtue* of memory,[53] and not just the faculty of memory. The virtue of memory is a cognitive integral part[54] of prudence, in which one has knowledge of the past,[55] since knowledge of the past is taken as proof of what could happen in the future.[56] As mentioned, experience is required to acquire memories[57] and prudence requires many memories.[58] The more memories one has, the more prudent one can be, since he will have more particulars[59] from which to consider possible future outcomes of circumstances and actions. It was already mentioned above how it is not just one's own personal

---

[52]The potential parts shall be discussed in the next section of this chapter.

[53]That memory is an integral part, see I-II, q. 57, a. 6, ad 4 and II-II, q. 48, a. 1.

[54]Ibid.

[55]Ibid.

[56]ST II-II, q. 49, a. 1, ad 3.

[57]III Sent., d. 33, q. 3, a. 1a and ST II-II, q. 49, a. 1. See also Aristotle's *Metaphysics* (980b29).

[58]ST II-II, q. 49, a. 1.

[59]See ibid., ad 1.

memories, but the collective experience and memories of the Church through its entire tradition that tell us what we should keep in mind theologically, in discussions of the nature of man, the virtue of religion, etc., when considering any liturgical change.

Through a good habit of memory, *i.e.*, by remembering the right things, we are less likely to suffer wonder (*admiratio*), and therefore, we will be less bound in our action when something unaccustomed arises.[60] By willing to remember, we can better order our considerations of prudential matters.[61] When we meditate on what we remember, thereby building the habit of memory, we are more able to know quickly what to do from what we remember.[62] Yet, what is important to see is that if one does not have a good habit of memory, one will not act prudently. When the Church considers changes or even how the pope must morally proceed in relation to the liturgy, if one discounts, ignores, or rejects the tradition which is the collective memory of the Church, imprudence is bound to occur.

The next thing required for a proper habit of memory is due solicitude. Memory helps one to take due solicitude since the experiences are impressed upon memory.[63] When we have a proper habit of memory, our memory will bring to mind those things which will move us to take due care and concern of those things which we ought. In fact, we often see the opposite: when someone forgets about the chicken he put in the oven, he will not do the "prudent" thing and remove the chicken from the oven when it is done cooking. Instead the chicken burns and only upon smelling the smoke does he remove

---

[60]Ibid., ad 2.

[61]Ibid.

[62]Ibid., ad 2.

[63]ST II-II, q. 49, a. 1, ad 2. In this passage, St. Thomas observes that the experiences are pressed upon the soul, but here we would understand that to mean memory, either sensitive or intellective.

it. Conversely, if a person gets in the habit of remembering things which he knows he should, the habit will aid him at the times when he needs to know those things necessary for prudential action. Again, this is why a pope cannot disregard the past, but must actively know and remember the tradition in order to act prudently, not just in regard to the liturgy, but in all ecclesial matters.

Due solicitude requires that the person knows when he should give his concern to some thing.[64] We should not have solicitude about things which are irrelevant or when it is not a suitable time for considering them. Solicitude implies a certain study which one employs to come to knowledge of something.[65] We tend to give greater study when there is fear of failing[66] and those who seek to be prudent must give due care to their consideration of those things which can affect their future actions. St. Thomas delineates four things which can make solicitude illicit regarding temporal matters:

> First, we must not constitute our end in them,[67] nor serve God for the sake of the necessities of food and clothes. ...Secondly, we must not be so solicitous about temporal matters, as to despair of divine aid.[68] ...Thirdly, the solicitude must not be presumptuous, as when man is confident to be able to procure the necessities of life without God's help. ...Fourth, man busies himself about the time of solicitude when he is solicitous now of something which does not pertain to the care of the present

---

[64]See ST II-II, q. 57, a. 7.

[65]ST II-II, q. 55, a. 6.

[66]Ibid.

[67]See ibid.

[68]See ibid.

time but to the care of the future.[69]

In another place, St. Thomas gives an additional reason why solicitude may be illicit: "solicitude for temporal things is able to be illicit, because of the excessive study which is given to procuring temporal goods, since man ought to serve more principally spiritual things."[70] As contained within these passages, we see that our primary concern must be about spiritual matters and only secondarily about temporal matters. Yet due solicitude is required on our part even for temporal matters, but it must be moderated by the understanding of when solicitude regarding temporal matters is illicit. These observations give pause to anyone researching the discussion about the changes in the Church in the 1960s. The "embracing the modern world," at times by some authors at least, appears to indicate that the primary concern was with the temporal and not the spiritual.

Prudence is of two kinds: supernatural and natural. Supernatural prudence has God as its end, and when considering the liturgy, because it is, as was seen in the last chapter, primarily concerned about the worship of God, it must always proceed from supernatural prudence and not natural or carnal prudence. Supernatural prudence orders supernatural means to a supernatural end, not a natural means to a supernatural end. As was noted above,

---

[69]ST I-II, q.108, a. 3, ad 5: "Primo qui dem, ut in eis finem non constituamus, neque Deo serviamus propter necessaria victus et vestitus. ...Secundo, ut non sic sollicitemur de temporalibus, cum desperatione divini auxilii. ... Tertio, ne sit sollicitudo praesumptuosa, ut scilicet homo confidat se necessaria vitae per suam sollicitudinem posse procurare, absque divino auxilio. ...Quarto, per hoc quod homo sollicitudinis tempus praeoccupat, quia scilicet de hoc sollicitus est nunc, quod non pertinet ad curam praesentis temporis, sed ad curam futuri."

[70]ST II-II, q. 55, a. 6: ."...Potest esse temporalium sollicitudo illicita propter superfluum studium quod apponitur ad temporalia procuranda, propter quod homo a spiritualibus, quibus principalius inservire debet, retrahitur"

the means must be proportionate to the end. If liturgical changes are made with worldliness or natural prudence and considerations in mind, the means will not be proportionate to the end (God). It will quickly devolve to being anthropocentric, since that is what worldliness or natural prudence primarily considers.

The habit or virtue of memory has three opposites. First, when a person does not remember things that he should, he suffers from the vice of forgetfulness. While forgetfulness can be from a purely physiological cause, it can also be volitional. Those who lead a life of the passions tend to suffer from precipitation and inconsideration, manifesting a lack of judgment and counsel which require remembering. Hence, those who lead a life of the passions will slowly fall into a vice of forgetfulness. Since remembering takes a certain amount of "psychological energy," those who lead a life of the passions will tend to find the virtue of memory distasteful, since it requires them to overcome the complacency of the passions in not remembering. This vice affects all considerations of prudence and that is why the virtue of memory is an integral part of prudence.

The distastefulness can also be when the things that should be remembered are painful or are contrary to one's passions. With anyone involved in making recommendations, or in the case of a pope who is making judgments about what should or should not be in the liturgy, if he suffers from forgetfulness, he is bound to make mistakes. This applies not only to his own personal life, but also if he volitionally "forgets" or ignores the memory of the Church, known through tradition.

The second opposite to the virtue of memory is when a person remembers the wrong things. A virtue is a good habit which means that the virtue of memory will move a person to remember the right things at the right time. This can likewise happen when prudence is involved in making decisions about the liturgy. If one remembers only certain things from the tradition or "remembers" them in a fashion that is not in congruity with the way they actually occurred, this can lead to errors in prudential judgment about liturgical change. One of the common phenomenon that was seen over the course of the past century when the liturgical studies and movement began, was that the knowledge of the tradition was very limited, and so false or wrong conclusions were drawn about the particular liturgical practices in the past. In more recent years, as the liturgical investigations were done in a more thorough way, the opposite conclusion was often discovered to be the case.

The third opposite to the virtue of memory is the vice of negligence. We have already mentioned it somewhat above, but it should be observed that this vice occurs when someone volitionally forgets or fails to remember things that he knows he should. This vice arises because of a lack of due solicitude and consideration of experiences. Essentially speaking, a person is going to be prudent when he is thoughtful and prone to contemplation. If a person finds these distasteful, he will be prone to forgetting things because he will not consider them. As the person brings the images of his experience to his imagination often, the memory and cogitative power are habituated to remember those things under the formality that reason places on them during consideration or contemplation of them. One who is negligent in remembering is bound to lapse into imprudence. In this respect, judgments about liturgical change not based on the tradition fall into the same problems, as is seen when one volitionally does not remember certain things of the tradition, because they may be contrary to one's appetites or passions.

B. Understanding (*Intellectus*)

Understanding is a cognitive[71] integral part[72] of prudence and is sometimes known as intelligence (*intelligentia*).[73] It is not to be

[71]ST II-II, q. 48, a. 1.

[72]Ibid. and ST I-II, q. 57, a. 6, ad 4.

[73]ST II-II, q. 48, a. 1 and ST I-II, q. 57, a. 6, ad 4.

misunderstood as the intellectual virtue of understanding, the connatural habit *intellectus principiorum*, nor the first act of the possible intellect of understanding. Rather, this is a practical virtue which gives a person knowledge of the present, either contingent or necessary.[74] This virtue gives one the ability to grasp the current state of affairs as they truly are. It gives the person knowledge not just of universal principles in general, but of which universal principles apply in a given case.[75] For this reason, St. Thomas says that understanding gives one a right estimation of a particular end[76] and this means that, in a particular situation, the person grasps (understands) the nature of the situation and knows which end is to be achieved, given the circumstances. He knows this end by applying universal knowledge to the concrete situation through understanding. The whole process of prudence is derived from understanding.[77]

Yet, St. Thomas makes an interesting observation which affects the application of the universal principles. He says that understanding helps one to judge not the proper sensibles, but the interior sense of the particular.[78] What this means is that the person grasps the end to be achieved based upon what the interior senses tell the person. This is very important because, since virtue lies in the mean relative to the individual, the person only knows what he should strive for (the particular end) when he judges it in light of both his exterior experience and his interior state. For example, if an alcoholic judges not on what his interior senses tell him but upon the

---

[74]III Sent., d. 33, q. 3, a. 1a and ST II-II, q. 48, a. 1

[75]See III Sent., d. 33, q. 3, a. 1a, ad 1 and Prummer, *Manuale Theologiae Moralis*, vol. 1, p. 458.

[76]ST II-II, q. 49, a. 2, ad 1 and ibid., a. 3.

[77]ST II-II, q. 49, a. 2.

[78]Ibid., ad 3.

consideration of alcohol in itself which is good, he will not judge based upon his past negative experience retained by his memory and assessed and prepared for abstraction by the cogitative power. Understanding gives the person the ability to look at the situation, judge himself interiorly based upon his own personal past experience, and then know for what end he must strive. This judgment then acts as a principle which determines the subsequent ratiocinative process of reason regarding what is to be done, *i.e.*, it is the principle which determines the process of counsel.

Obviously, when liturgical changes are contemplated, a true grasp of reality as well as one's own interior state are paramount. Moreover, one must also be able to judge the current state of affairs in the interior lives of the faithful as they truly are, and not through the lens of elation or rose-colored glasses. The fact that in the last century the interior lives of the faithful varied drastically, the liturgical changes should have been slow and few in coming to avoid any destabilization of the view the faithful had of the faith, especially at a time when two world wars had been fought and cultural and societal stability was in question.

C. Docility (*Docilitas*)

Docility is a cognitive,[79] integral part[80] of prudence in which one acquires knowledge by learning from another.[81] One man cannot know all of the particulars which a person can encounter in life. So he needs to be taught by others, especially the elderly who have a healthy understanding about the ends of acts.[82] Essentially, this virtue makes

---

[79]ST II-II, q. 48, a 1.

[80]Ibid. and ST I-II, q. 57, a. 6, ad 4. See also ST II-II, q. 49, a. 3.

[81]ST II-II, q. 48, a. 1.

[82]ST II-II, q. 49, a. 3.

one receptive to learning[83] from others. Those who can learn from the good acts and the mistakes of others as well as from the general knowledge of others are more likely to act prudently. This is because they can store the other person's counsel in memory and use it when appropriate circumstances arise. The aptitude to docility is from nature, but its completion is from human study, in which the person applies himself to the great documents and texts, frequently, reverently and with care, not neglecting them out of ignorance nor despising them because of pride.[84] In the context of the liturgy, it is imperative that those who are entrusted with its care, especially the pope, be docile to the "elders," and in this case elders is another name for the saints, Fathers of the Church, Doctors of the Church, and past popes. In effect, his docility must be to the tradition, since it is in the tradition that the wisdom and knowledge of the Church and her past experience with liturgical development resides.

If a person is not willing to learn from the great and prudent writers of the past, he is unlikely to be able to achieve a more developed virtue of prudence. While the common man can watch others, avoid pitfalls by following their example, and even from time to time ask another's counsel, greatness of prudence requires a thorough knowledge of universal principles as well as how those principles have been applied throughout history. Knowledge of those of a single lifetime is not as great as knowledge accumulated by great authors over centuries. Man is able to be more prudent when he relies on the wisdom of the ages, rather than on mere contemporary wisdom.[85] In relation to theological matters, the first principles are the articles of the Creed,[86] but one may also say by extension the totality

[83]ST II-II, q. 49, a. 3.

[84]Ibid., ad 2.

[85]This is why tradition is so important.

[86]ST I, q. 1, a. 7.

of the Church's Sacred Tradition. In regard to liturgical development, the docility is perfected when those in charge of its development have a thorough knowledge of the tradition as to its theological content as well as observance of the Church's past experience in dealing with liturgical change, for both good and bad.

Docility requires a certain discernment of judgment, since one must choose wisely those from whom one takes counsel. This may be difficult, but one of the ways one does so is by observing other men and how they conduct their lives. If a particular man seems virtuous and prudent, docility should be more readily given to him than someone who is not prudent. There is a false docility among those who, knowing their sin or adherence to heresy, will choose to take counsel from only certain aspects of the tradition, which they know will confirm them in their disorder. Historically, this has been seen in certain theologians where they will be very selective regarding liturgical texts or commentary from the tradition to the exclusion of others, in order to promote a narrative in congruity with their theological error or disordered appetites. To put it plainly, heretics are selective[87] about the aspects of the tradition that they follow.

D. Shrewdness (*Solertia*)

Shrewdness[88] is a cognitive, integral part[89] of prudence, sometimes called *eustochia*. Shrewdness is a skill or quickness of mind

---

[87]Heresy comes from the Greek term αἱρέω which means choice.

[88]The term *solertia* does not seem to have a good English counterpart, since shrewdness sometimes has a negative connotation. However, the use of the term shrewdness here does not imply anything negative but, quite the contrary, it is a positive designation. Deferrari, in *A Latin-English Dictionary of St. Thomas* (p. 979), translates *solertia* as shrewdness, skill, and quickness of mind.

[89]ST II-II, q. 48, a. 1.

in discovering something, especially the principle of a thing.[90] Eustochia is "the capability or virtue of good conjecture[91] or guessing in practical things."[92] Shrewdness is a quickness[93] at finding[94] or conjecturing about the means to the end.[95] St. Thomas observes that it is a kind of subtlety or ease of conjecturing the means[96] and it depends more on a natural genius, than from custom.[97] Prummer defines shrewdness as "a prompt conjecture about the congruent means to some intended end to be obtained or shrewdness is a certain perspicacity quickly apprehending the means, which happens from natural aptitude or also from exercise."[98] Prummer goes on in the same location to observe that shrewdness is by degrees, since it is based upon a natural gift, even though it can be developed through exercise. Essentially, this means that some people are simply quicker at knowing which means will lead to a given end in a particular set of circumstances, either by natural ability or by habit (exercise).

---

[90]See Deferrari, loc. cit.

[91]III Sent., d. 33, q. 3, a. 1d; ST II-II, q. 48, a. 1 and ibid., q. 49, a. 4.

[92]Deferrari, *A Latin-English Dictionary of St. Thomas*, p. 363.

[93]III Sent., d. 33, q. 3, a. 1d; ST II-II, q. 49, a. 4 and ibid., ad 4.

[94]ST II-II, q. 48, a.1 and ibid., q. 49, a. 4.

[95]ST II-II, q. 48, a.1 and ibid., q. 49, a. 4. See also In Ethic., VI, l. 8 (n. 1219).

[96]*In Libros Posteriororum Analyticorum*, I, l. 44, n. 12.

[97]III Sent., d. 33, q. 3, a. 1d.

[98]Prummer, *Manuale Theologiae Moralis*, vol. 1, p. 458: "est prompta coniectura circa media congruentia ad aliquem finem intentum obtinendum, seu sollertia est quaedam perspicacitas velociter apprehendendi medium, quae contingit ex naturali aptitudine et etiam ex exercitio."

Liturgically, especially in regard to saints, there are certain people who simply have a natural sense of what is suitable and what is not, and so they can often quickly arrive at the best liturgical development as regards a specific aspect of the liturgy. This is not to be confused with precipitation or inconsideration which will be discussed below, which often occurs in liturgical discussions, even on a historical basis. The liturgical changes made by the Protestants were largely a matter of indocility, precipitation, inconsideration, and immemory (lack of memory) regarding the tradition due to appetitive distaste for all things Catholic.[99] Even now in the Church, after 50 years of liturgical change, the discussion about what should be done in the liturgy is fraught with an adherence to the status quo and an inability to realize that many of the liturgies offered today are rife with serious difficulties. Intellectual blindness and other vices can impede or slow the intellectual judgment about what is suitable liturgically.

E. Reason (*Ratio*)

Reason or reasoning is a cognitive[100] integral part[101] of prudence in which one proceeds from the knowledge he has to other knowledge or judgments.[102] Sometimes called good reasoning,[103] reason is the ability to apply universals to particulars well.[104] In the discussion of the practical syllogism, how the universal is applied in

---

[99]For a discussion of the changes made by the Protestants after the reformation, see Davies, *Cranmer's Godly Order*.

[100]ST II-II, q. 48, a. 1.

[101]Ibid. and ST II-II, q. 49, a. 5.

[102]ST II-II, q. 48, a. 1.

[103]ST II-II, q. 49, a. 5.

[104]Ibid., ad 2.

the concrete by the recognition of the middle term and its proper distribution, is key.[105] Reason, the integral part of prudence, aids the person in being able to do precisely that.

Some people have a good ability to grasp universal principles, such as that retributive justice demands that one pay back what one has stolen. But as to the actual application in the concrete, they may have great difficulties, *e.g.*, moral theologians indicate that one does not have to pay back the person from whom one has taken money, if there is some grave harm that would come to the person who has stolen the property. But those who lack the integral part of prudence of reason will find that they have a hard time applying the principles of retributive justice, because they have a hard time seeing the principles embodied in the circumstances. As a result, they may cause themselves harm by giving money back to their boss, for example, and then they are fired because of it.

What blocks the process of reason is the lack of a proper grasp of the circumstances, as well as a lack of intellectual habits to be able to apply the right principles, even when one does know the circumstances. Both of these can pose problems with liturgical development. If a group of people are wed to the world or do not have a proper grasp of the age in which they live, they are likely to not be able to quickly see what needs to be done, but are more likely to be blocked in their reasoning process, since they will not judge rightly which principles apply in the concrete. Furthermore, this is precisely why knowledgeable saints should be entrusted with liturgical development. Aside from the reality that they normally grasp the circumstances and age in which they live, due to their appetites being subdued by virtue, they also have often studied the theological principles to a much greater depth, and due to the proper virtue (which gives clear phantasms by which the concrete circumstances are

---

[105]See Ripperger, *Introduction to the Science of Mental Health*, vol. I, p. 88 for a discusison of distribution as to its nature and ibid., vol. III, pt. 2, chpt. 1, p. 722 for its application to prudence in the practical syllogism.

known) as well as profound theological knowledge (the virtue of science), their ability to quickly see what does not fit the liturgy is clear, and their ability to know what does fit is more likely and quicker than those who are not knowledgeable saints.

F. Foresight (*Providentia*)

Foresight is a preceptive,[106] integral part[107] of prudence by which one applies knowledge to action[108] by ordering action to a suitable end.[109] Foresight implies distance,[110] *i.e.*, the person with foresight is able to see how a given action will achieve a future end. St. Thomas says that foresight is a more principal part than the other parts, since all the parts of prudence are necessary so that one can order the means to the end which is seen by foresight.[111] St. Thomas says that the name of prudence comes from providence or foresight (*prudentia*/*providentia*)[112] and foresight occurs when something future is seen by the person before it is done[113] or before it happens, and he is able to foresee any obstacles so that they may be removed.[114] It is a kind of prescience or foreknowledge in which a person can read the

---

106 ST II-II, q. 48, a. 1.

107 Ibid. and ST I-II, q. 57, a. 6, ad 4.

108 ST II-II, q. 48, a. 1.

109 Ibid.

110 ST II-II, q. 49, a. 6.

111 Ibid., ad 1.

112 Ibid.

113 III Sent., d. 33, q. 3, a. 1a.

114 III Sent., d. 33, q. 3, a. 1b.

circumstances and know what would happen, if various actions should be tried in those particular circumstances.

The difference between shrewdness and foresight is that shrewdness is a quickness at the process of conjecturing, whereas foresight is the ability to foresee through the conjecturing, what will happen. So one is the quickness of mind while the other is the actual vision into the future. Prummer observes that foresight is taken in two ways, *viz.*, (1) for the ordination of the means to the end and (2) for the consideration of future events.[115] The ordination of the means to the end is why this part is a preceptive part of prudence rather than a mere cognitive part of prudence, even though it does require a knowledge or ability to see intellectually what outcomes will come from the various causes and circumstances in a given case. It is preceptive because foresight commands or orders the means toward a future end.

Any proposed liturgical change or development should only be done by a man who has sufficient foresight, *i.e.*, he needs to be able to grasp what is likely to happen when a change is envisioned, as well as looking at the circumstances and knowing which liturgical change is likely to not just affect in a positive manner those of the time but even in the future. In a certain sense, supernatural foresight when applied to the liturgy would know whether a change is time bound, and therefore, likely to fail long term, or is likely to stand the test of time in the future and become timeless or perennial in the proper sense. In this respect, only those who have a highly developed supernatural foresight should have any involvement in the liturgical development.

St. Thomas says that foresight is impeded in three ways.[116]

---

[115]Prummer, *Manuale Theologiae Moralis*, vol. 1, p. 459.

[116]III Sent., d. 33, q. 3, a. 1b: "Uno modo ex parte ipsius viae inveniendae, quae quandoque videtur bona, et non est; et hoc impedimentum cautio aufert, cujus est ex virtutibus vitia virtutum speciem praeferentia discernere.

> In one way on the part of the way of finding, which sometimes seems good but is not. Caution removes this impediment, of which it is to discern from the virtues the preference of the species of virtue to vice.

Foresight can be affected when something appears good to a person when it is not. If a person develops a preference for virtue and keeps that in his mind when considering what should be done, he will judge what should be done based upon whether it will attain virtue or whether the proposed course of action proceeds from vice. When proposed changes or development of the liturgy is considered, any individual who has not mastered his antecedent appetite or is prone to elation regarding the age in which he lives should automatically be excluded.

> In another way, from the very order to the end; either the way is not of itself apt to the end, or it is impeded by something extrinsic so that it is not able to lead to the end; and this pertains to circumspection, which is caution of contrary vices by which prudence especially is impeded.

Sometimes foresight is impeded by something extrinsic to the agent. If a person is incircumspect, he does not keep track of those things outside of him or around him and so his proposed action will not take into account external impediments. Sometimes, the very means by its nature will not achieve the end.

Alio modo ex ordine ipsius in finem, ne scilicet via quae de se apta est ad finem, aliquo extrinseco impediatur ne in finem ducere possit; et hoc ad circumspectionem pertinet, quae est cautela vitiorum contrariorum, quibus praecipue prudentia impeditur. Tertio modo ex parte ipsius hominis tendentis in finem, qui vias accommodas ad finem intentum invenire non potest: unde oportet quod per doctrinam ab aliis accipiat. Quia oportet principia operabilia vel a se habere prudentem, vel ab alio faciliter accipere. Qui autem neutrum habet, hic inutilis est vir."

> In a third way, on the part of the very man tending to the end, who is not able to find suitable ways to the intended end: hence it is necessary that he receives through teaching from others. Since it is necessary regarding the operative principles that either he has prudence from himself or he easily receives it from another. He who has neither, is a useless man.[117]

In this case, a man's very own lack of the operative principles affects his ability to be prudent, so he must get them from another. Without operative principles, or to put it another way, unless a man is a principled man, he simply will not be prudent. A man may not be principled for two reasons. Either he simply does not know the principles, *i.e.*, the psychological constitution of man[118] or he is unwilling or unable to apply the principles in the concrete. If a person has no principles, he will not have foresight because he will not know what is going to happen, or if he knows what will happen, he may not know whether it is good or bad for him morally or psychologically. If he lacks the ability to apply the principles in the concrete, *i.e.*, he lacks the integral part of reason, he will not have foresight because he will not know if certain principles or actions will produce certain future events by the application of the principles in the concrete. All of this tells us that while foresight is the more principal part of prudence, foresight itself depends on the other principal parts for its operation.

A man who is not principled will never be a good liturgist. This is for more than one reason. The first is that since the articles of the Creed, *i.e.*, what we believe as Catholics, constitute the principles

---

[117]St. Thomas then goes on to discuss how docility is necessary for the person in this situation.

[118]If a person follows the moral code of the Catholic Church which embodies a following and developing of all of the virtues, the person is more likely to be prudent and not have mental illness. The moral code of the Catholic Church is founded upon and takes into full consideration the ontological structure of man and its proper operation.

that guide liturgical action, then if he is not principled, his liturgical activity simply will not be Catholic. The second reason is that a man who is not principled, in the current historical context, is likely to be a modernist. This follows from the fact that a modernist does not take reality as the foundation for what he believes, but rather the principle of immanence. He will judge what he wants to do liturgically, not based on theological principle, which is known in reality, but upon his own ideas, the quality of his experience of things, his emotions, etc. In the end, he will conform the liturgy to himself as the end, rather than ordering it to God as the end. His foresight will be that of carnal prudence and not even natural or supernatural prudence. For example, when it comes to the consideration of which direction will he offer the Holy Sacrifice, he is more likely to face the people (*i.e.*, man), and not God (traditionally considered symbolically in the east).[119]

G. Circumspection (*Circumspectio*)

Circumspection is a preceptive,[120] integral part[121] of prudence in which one applies knowledge to action.[122] Knowledge here concerns the circumstances of the action and so circumspection compares the end which one wants to achieve and the circumstances

[119]It should be recognized that many of the bishops and priests face the people out of a sense of obedience and not out of modernist tendencies.

[120]ST II-II, q. 48, a. 1. It is not completely clear why this is a preceptive part rather than a cognitive part, other than the possibility that prudence requires that the person execute the action when the circumstances are right; see infra this paragraph. The fact that the person must command the action in due circumstances may be why it is a preceptive integral part rather than merely a cognitive integral part.

[121]Ibid.

[122]Ibid.

in which one finds oneself to see if the end fits the circumstances.[123] For example, a child might need disciplining, but the public place in which a parent finds himself indicates that this is not the place where it should be done.

In another work, we observed several things in relation to circumspection. First, it was noted that passions affect circumspection.[124] Since passions affect the phantasm, they affect the judgment of the singular (circumstances as represented in the phantasm). This is why all emotionalism must be absolutely excluded from prudential considerations in relation to the liturgy. Any liturgical action designed to feed the emotions of the faithful or priest is inherently going to be imprudent due to the fact that the proper object of the passions is not God, but some created good. While God can be considered emotionally, the emotions reduce it down to a natural activity or consideration, rather than it being something pertaining to the faith (intellect), hope, or charity (the will).

Second, if a child is raised with right order within the family (proper circumstances for psychological health), he will learn circumspection.[125] This essentially means that a rightly ordered environment aids the child in judgment of singulars which will have an appreciable effect on his prudence. Having parents who are virtuous (also a circumstance of the child) will directly affect the child's judgment. In the context of the Church, how the pope and bishops direct the liturgy to be done has a direct impact on the circumspection of the faithful. If the faithful observe the clergy offering Mass reverently and according to the laws of the Church, they will grasp which circumstances fit the liturgical actions and which do not. The

---

[123]ST II-II, q. 49, a. 7 and ibid., ad 3.

[124]See Ripperger, *Introduction to the Science of Mental Health*, volume one, chapter nine (IV).

[125]See ibid., volume one, chapter thirteen (II).

often repeated criticism of the ancient form of Mass before Vatican II is that the priest said it sloppily, hastily, without clean vessels or linens, etc. But these are all circumstances and not the substance of the liturgy. To suggest that the lack of virtue on the side of the clergy would demand a change in the ritual is like suggesting that, since no one lives Christianity or the moral code of the Catholic faith perfectly, it should be substantially revised.

Third, it was observed that those who lose chastity will lose the more subtle virtues such as circumspection.[126] The subtlety of the virtue of circumspection is based upon the fact that passion draws one into an interior consideration of one's appetitive state. In other words, a person, through passion, is taken out of his contact with reality, of which the circumstances are a part. For this reason, highly developed circumspection is a sign of mental health (contact with reality) and/or virtue. Without a proper moral life and especially chastity, one will not act prudently, and therefore, simply will not know the proper courses of action. Yet, quietly, it was becoming very clear to the authorities in the Church that there was a serious problem of lack of chastity in the seminaries and among the clergy. The very fact that the Sacred Congregation For Religious published the document *Religiosorum Institutio* in February of 1961, calling attention to the problem of lack of chastity in the seminaries and religious life, indicates that the 1960s was a time when circumspection about the good and bad of the times would not have been properly in place. In fact, we also know now due to the pedophilia scandal, where many of the cases of abuse took place in the 1970s and 1980s, it was because the priests who committed them were in the seminaries in the 1950s and 1960s. The call for large scale changes in the liturgy at that time was a sign of incircumspection. Since the liturgy requires interior discipline, self denial, and sacrifice in order to offer it in a manner pleasing to God, changing the liturgy at a time when there was a lack of interior self control was bound to lead to problems. While it is difficult to track the

---

[126]See ibid., volume two, chapter six (III).

original source of the quote, it is nonetheless still true: "self abuse leads to liturgical abuse and liturgical abuse leads to self abuse."

H. Caution (*Cautio*)

Caution is a preceptive,[127] integral part[128] of prudence by which one applies knowledge to action[129] in order to avoid impediments[130] and evils.[131] Caution differs from providence, because caution deals with evils and their avoidance, whereas providence deals with the good, *i.e.*, achieving the end. St. Thomas says that caution is an adjunct to contrition[132] and by this he means that when a person is sorry for his sin, he will be cautious in the future so that he can avoid the sin and not be sorry for more sin. Obviously we see the connection between caution and Fear of the Lord. Caution is a virtue or action lying in a mean. The danger is in the extremes: when the person is not cautious enough or when he is too cautious.

When liturgical development is governed by prudence, a proper caution is observed. Historically, this came in the form of only slight changes made to the liturgy over a long period of time, *i.e.*, the process was slow to ensure that nothing bad happened and prudence was observed. Moreover, during a time of moral collapse or during a time of heresy, the changes to be made should be slow, if at all. In fact, after the Protestant revolt, the Church did make changes, but a careful observation will reveal that it was more a case of codification

---

[127]ST II-II, q. 48, a. 1.

[128]Ibid. and ST I-II, q. 57, a. 6, ad 4.

[129]ST II-II, q. 48, a. 1.

[130]Ibid. and *Super Ephesios*, c. 5, l. 6.

[131]ST II-II, q. 49, a. 8.

[132]IV Sent., d. 17, q. 2, a. 2d.

of what was present in the liturgical tradition. In effect, it was a "lock down" of sorts, which did continue to develop organically in the subsequent centuries through additions to the calendar, etc., but the lock down was to avoid heresy creeping into the liturgy.

Caution is obviously connected to the Gift of the Holy Spirit of Fear of the Lord. This gift essentially inclines one to have reverence for God and a desire to, and seeking of not offending Him. As was seen in a prior chapter, the fact that God was very specific about *how* He was to be worshiped indicates that human beings with reason affected by the darkness of the intellect of original and actual sin, and given the history of humanity when men try to determine how God is to be worshiped are very prone to introducing into the worship of God things that are offensive to Him. In the end, it is *God* Who must tell us how He is to be worshiped. It is not the place of the creature (due circumspection required) to determine how he relates to God and how God will be worshiped. The very fact that God came down and gave detailed instructions to Moses on the ceremonies and the fact that Christ said, "do *this* in commemoration of me," the "this" is a clear indicator that He is setting the parameters of the worship. Hence, historically, the changes suggested were often done by the saints who were men of God and knew the mind of God. The fact that today we allow men who struggle with the *graviora delicta* to make liturgical suggestions lacks any semblance of circumspection or caution. It cannot be seen as anything other than gravely imprudent. The pope himself would promulgate these changes making sure that priest and faithful alike learned that the determination of the liturgy was a top down structure, not a bottom up. This is why only saintly popes or popes who followed the tradition and suggestions of saintly men had involvement in the liturgical process of authentic development.

Furthermore, to speak plainly, the Church in her wisdom also knew that men were intellectually daft and that the clergy could not be trusted to determine what was in the liturgy, because they simply were not that bright or virtuous. To put it another way, if you let the priests make the determinations about what is in the liturgy, dumb choices are going to be made. No citation is necessary to support this observation. Any Catholic who has been to Mass and follows the news in the Church knows this absolutely to be the case, not just from what they have read in the news, but by their own personal experience in sitting through liturgies that defy imagination. Hence, once the early Church period and the persecutions were over, the liturgical development quickly solidified the liturgical action, and by the time of St. Gregory the Great and the codification of the liturgy by 604,[133] the Church had taken out of the hands of the priest the determination of the choices of what was going to be in the daily liturgy. In the ancient form of Mass, there were options, but under strict circumstances, and once the options were chosen, the flow of the Mass was determined. This is necessary as a matter of basic prudence, or we may say, it is the proper effect of an elementary virtue of caution.

III. Potential Parts of Prudence

A. Good Counsel (*Eubulia*)

Potential parts of a virtue are those parts which do not fall directly under the virtue, but which are connected to the virtue by the matter about which they are concerned. The first subjective part[134] is the virtue of good counsel[135] or euboulia.[136] Euboulia, as the virtue of

---

[133]The exact dates of the codification seem to be unclear in the various historians this author consulted. What is known is that by St. Gregory's death in 604 the changes had been made.

[134]ST II-II, q. 48, a. 1.

[135]III Sent., d. 34, q. 1, a. 2; ibid., d. 35, q. 2, a. 4a; ST I, q. 22, a. 1 ad 1; ST I-II, q. 51, a. 1 and De Vir., q. 5, a. 1.

[136]For the sake of grammatical clarity, the term *euboulia* will be used instead of good counsel.

good counsel, is a certain inquisition[137] or finding of the means.[138] Through the virtue of euboulia, one is able to find a suitable means according to due time and other circumstances.[139] The difference between prudence and euboulia is that euboulia is about the process of taking counsel, whereas prudence is principally about commanding (preceptive) the right action.[140] All of the integral parts of prudence affect counsel, but are not counsel itself. Despite the distinction between euboulia or good counsel and prudence, euboulia is ordered toward prudence.[141] A further distinction is in order since above it was noted that there are three acts of prudence, *viz.*, counsel, judgment, and command. Counsel here is the act of counsel, not the virtue. The integral parts of prudence affect counsel but are not the virtues of counsel. Rather, counsel is a separate virtue since prudence is more preceptive, *i.e.*, more ordered toward commanding (executing action) than the discursive process of coming to know what should be done.

There are four conditions for euboulia.[142] The first is that it must be about the good. Since euboulia is a virtue and virtue is always about the good, the virtue of good counsel must always concern the good and not evil. Once evil enters the process of counsel as real

---

[137]In Ethic., VI, l. 8 (n. 1218).

[138]ST II-II, q. 47, a. 15, ad 1. The term for "means" is *ea quae sunt ad finem* which indicates that the means is not just the action which helps one attain the ends, but also the circumstances which are used to attain the end. For a lengthy discussion of this, see this author's two-part article, "The Morality of the Exterior Act" as found in the *Angelicum* (LXXVI [1999], pp. 183-220 and LXXVI [1999], pp. 267-410) or Ripperger, *The Morality of the Exterior Act.*

[139]III Sent., d. 33, q. 3, a. 1c.

[140]See ST II-II, q. 51, a. 2.

[141]See ST II-II, q. 51, a. 2.

[142]These are taken from In Ethic., VI, l. 8 (nn.1228-1233).

means, it ceases being an act of euboulia.[143] Hence, historically, when heretics would take over, their pertinacity in their heresy was the evil which guided their liturgical deliberations and their error was that to which they conformed their liturgical changes.

The second condition for euboulia is that it must proceed from a true syllogism to arrive at the means to the end. It was noted above that the integral parts of prudence and prudence itself deal with drawing a practical conclusion from a universal premise and a particular premise. A false syllogism will not follow logical rules and is, therefore, contrary to right reason. If it is contrary to right reason, it cannot be part of the virtue of good counsel which lies in the practical intellect as a subject. While it is true that sometimes people will stumble upon the right or even prudent thing to do from bad reasoning, nevertheless the bad reasoning itself is not a good form of counsel.

The third condition for euboulia to be present is that euboulia attends to that which is useful to the end to which a man ought to strive and according to a due mode and time. What this essentially means is that the virtue of good counsel considers (1) whether the action suits the end, (2) whether the circumstances fit the action and (3) whether the circumstances fit the end. Due mode and time are circumstances and so euboulia makes use of circumspection in order to reason properly about the means.[144]

The fourth condition for euboulia is that it must be directed to the good of the whole human life. It is not enough for the action to be

---

[143]This is why St. Thomas observes that euboulia is not found in sinners, since every sin is against good counsel; see ST II-II, q. 51, a. 1, ad 3. By sinners here is meant those in the state of mortal sin. While the natural virtue of euboulia may be in sinners, even if at times it is not employed, the infused virtue of euboulia is not, since one must be in the state of grace to have any of the infused virtues. That euboulia may be infused, see ibid., ad 1.

[144]For a discussion of suitability in relation to the liturgy, see Ripperger, *Topic on Tradition*, p. 186-193.

good here and now, without any reference to it being good for the person's whole life. A certain context must be kept intellectually to make sure that what the person may do in the concrete circumstances fits into a perspective which takes into account the effect this action will have on the person's entire life. It is not enough to satisfy oneself here and now, but one must look to see how this will affect one's whole life, which means how it will affect the achievement of his final end. Committing a mortal sin might help one save his home, but if the person dies before he gets to confession, the action was exceptionally imprudent.[145]

Supernatural euboulia has God as its object, just as all theological and infused virtues do. Since the liturgy is about God, then any consideration of liturgical change or development must proceed from supernatural euboulia. This is said in two ways. The first is that the pope himself must take his own supernatural counsel. His grace of office will supply him with the proper direction of that counsel, provided that he has a habit of being faithful to grace and not following his own will or appetites. Second, most popes consult knowledgeable theologians. These theologians must be known for the supernatural prudence with all of its integral parts. Moreover, any liturgy by committee is going to be excluded thereby, or at least cautioned against. This follows from the fact that saintly men are likely to agree on what liturgical changes are to be made, but having numerous theologians address one or two parts and then putting them all together to make up a whole liturgy does not appear prudent. There is no guarantee of suitability that one part will fit another unless there is one individual to judge all of the parts and how they relate. But then again, we are back to the principle of unity obtaining here, *i.e.*, governance (but also judication), can only be done by one individual or by individuals acting as a single agent.[146] But even in the

---

[145]It would be imprudent based purely on the fact that it offends God.

[146]See St. Thomas Aquinas, *De Regimine Principiis*, bk. I, chpt. II.

later case, one individual is directive of the other individuals. Furthermore, committees rarely are full of all virtuous men, and if an unscrupulous individual were to be directive of them, then any counsel given by that committee to the pope would be worthless at best, suspect, and disordered at worst. The process would be imprudent on virtually every level.

B. Synesis

Synesis[147] is a potential part[148] of prudence in which one judges those things which fall under and are according to the common law.[149] There are certain things which happen to a person that, when a person contemplates a course of action, he realizes that the judgment of the means falls under normal precepts, *e.g.*, if he drives off in another man's automobile he knows that it falls under the precept of "thou shalt not steal." Synesis judges the means and not the end.[150] There are three acts related to prudence, *viz.*, counsel, judgment (of the means), and command.[151] The act of counsel is affected by the integral parts of prudence as well as the virtue of counsel. The act of judgment of the means[152] is affected by the integral parts of prudence as well as by the

---

[147]There is no English correlating term to synesis. Most moralists simply use the term directly in English without any modification.

[148]ST II-II, q. 48, a. 1.

[149]III Sent., d. 33, q. 3, a. 1c, ad 3; ST I-II, q. 57, a. 6, ad 3; ST II-II, q. 48, a. 1; ibid., q. 51, a. 4 and ibid., ad 4. See also III Sent., d. 35, q. 2, a. 4b, ad 3.

[150]ST II-II, q. 51, a. 3, ad 1.

[151]These are three acts of the intellect which deal with the means regarding the decision-making process as delineated in volume one, chapter seven of Ripperger, *Introduction to the Science of Mental Health.*

[152]It should be observed that judgment of the means is a different act of the intellect in the decision-making process than judgment of the end.

virtue of synesis, when the action falls under the common law. St. Thomas notes that synesis helps one to grasp things as they are[153] and gives one a right judgment about the means.[154] For this reason, Deferrari defines synesis as "the virtue of common sense in practical affairs, *i.e.*, the habit of judging rightly about the practical individual cases according to the customary rules of life."[155] An example of synesis in relation to liturgical action would be the principle that Apostolicity was to be followed, and if it is clear that it came from the Apostles, albeit reported by the Fathers, the synesis would dictate that is what is to be done in the liturgy.

C. Gnome

Gnome[156] is a potential part in relation to prudence, and it is the virtue which judges of those things which recede from the common law.[157] Deferrari defines it as an aptitude[158] or ability to judge rightly over the extraordinary things of life."[159] Sometimes it happens

---

[153]ST II-II, q. 51, a. 3, ad 1.

[154]ST I, q. 22, a. 1, ad 1. See also ST II-II, q. 60, a. 1, ad 1.

[155]Deferrari in *A Latin-English Dictionary of St. Thomas*, p. 1026. In the same entry in Deferrari, he observes that synesis is better than euboulia, since the right judgment about the best means is better than taking counsel about all of the possible means.

[156]Like synesis, there is no English correlating term to gnome. Most moralists simply use the term directly in English without any modification.

[157]ST I-II, q. 57, a. 6, ad 3; ST II-II, q. 51, a. 4 and ST II-II, q. 80, a. 1, ad 4. See also De Vir., q. 5, a. 1.

[158]Gnome implies a certain perspicacity of judgment, see ST II-II, q. 51, a. 4 and ibid., ad 3.

[159]Deferrari in *A Latin-English Dictionary of St. Thomas*, p. 443.

to a person that the circumstances in which he finds himself are out of the ordinary and not common and so the virtue of gnome helps him to judge what to do according to "higher principles."[160] In *Prima Secundae*, St. Thomas indicates that the higher principles are the Natural Law itself.[161] This means that in order to exercise the virtue of gnome, a person has to have knowledge not just of general precepts, such as "thou shalt not steal" but about the very structure of human nature and the application of the Natural Law in concrete circumstances. If a man has a knowledge of the three categories of natural inclination and what falls under each category, he will have the ability to know what should be done in extraordinary circumstances. On the other hand, some who are very bright may have a decent grasp of human nature (and therefore what suits it, *i.e.*, the Natural Law) and know what to do in extraordinary circumstances.

The supernatural virtue of gnome would have God as its proper object and it would envision knowing the Divine Positive Law and the Natural Law in order to know what to do when the common law does not apply. For example, the ecclesiastical precept of the obligation to attend Mass on Sundays and Holy Days of Obligation is one in which synesis would judge normal circumstances to be present, and so the precept binds the person under the pain of mortal sin. However, if one is sick, the circumstance of the sickness would exempt one from the obligation to attend Mass. It is possible to envision a time in the Church, where the liturgical law would break down to such a degree, that members of the Magisterium incorporate things into the liturgy which no Catholic in conscience can participate in[162] or the like, and one would not be bound to fulfill one's obligation

---

[160]ST II-II, q. 51, a. 4.

[161]ST I-II, q. 57, a. 6, ad 3.

[162]Examples would be the incorporation of the Pachamama or native American rituals which are contrary to the faith.

in those circumstances. The virtue of gnome would help one to make proper judgments about which principles of the Natural Law and Divine Positive Law apply. If a person lives in an area where there is only one parish within 60 minutes of travel time[163] and the local pastor gravely abuses the liturgy, the Divine Positive Law would indicate that one must preserve one's Catholic faith over attending Mass, if it were to become an impediment to one's faith.

IV. Certain Vices contrary to Prudence

In order to get a more rounded view of prudence and its application to the liturgy, it would behoove the discussion to consider certain vices into which people fall, which are contrary to prudence as they apply to liturgical change and development.

A. Precipitation

Imprudence has four species, *viz.*, precipitation, inconsideration, inconstancy, and negligence.[164] The first species of imprudence is precipitation. Counsel is about how the means and the passion of lust precipitates or destroys counsel[165] and so one is unable to "rule," insofar as to rule implies guiding something to an end.[166] When someone lacks counsel, he is affected in his ability to discern the various means he could employ to arrive at his proper end. Precipitation, then, is a defect of counsel[167] in which one does not take

---

[163]In the past in most moral manuals, one hour of travel time exempted one from the obligation to hear Mass.

[164]Prummer, *Manuale Theologiae Moralis*, vol. 1, p. 460.

[165]ST II-II, q. 53, aa. 2 and 6 and ibid., q. 53, a. 3, ad 3.

[166]How the passions cause precipitation, see Ripperger, *Introduction to the Science of Mental Health*, vol. I, chpt. 9.

[167]ST II-II, q. 53, aa. 2 and 5.

adequate counsel, or the act of counsel fails due to passion clouding the judgment of reason. Precipitation is a failing in one or more of the following areas.[168] It is a failing in docility when the person's judgment is affected in such a way that he does not take counsel from another when he should. Sometimes precipitation is caused by passions other than lust, *e.g.*, fear.

While the pope is not subject to the Cardinals or the bishops, he should take counsel from the various bishops and Cardinals. If they have grave cause about a liturgical change, he should give that sufficient consideration and weight. As a general rule, he would not normally act upon his own, even though he would have the authority to do so, when it would go contrary to a majority of orthodox bishops and Cardinals. It would be contrary to prudence, insofar as it would be precipitous for the pope to make the changes contrary to the grasping of the circumstances, which would include gaining a knowledge of what the Cardinals and the bishops judged regarding the matter. Here he would have to avoid only taking the counsel of those who agreed with him, but taking into consideration all of those bishops, who were orthodox, *i.e.*, held to the orthodox Catholic faith.

Precipitation may also be due to a failure in memory. Sometimes passions bind the various faculties and so the faculty of memory and the cogitative power cannot recall those things which would affect one's judgment. For instance, an alcoholic would be precipitous if, when he saw a bottle of wine, he immediately began trying to open it without remembering the bad experiences he has had when he has gotten drunk. This is precisely why any kind of liturgical augmentation or change would have to take into consideration the entire tradition of the Church. It is precisely through the tradition of the Church that the Church's experiences reveal when things turned out badly, when they turned out well, and when they could have been improved. But to simply ignore the entire tradition of the Church, or to ignore the bad effects of liturgical change, and to propose those

---

[168]See ST II-II, q. 53, a. 2.

same liturgical changes, when they turned out badly in the past, would be precipitous.

Precipitation may also be due to a failure in reason. Since the soul is held bound by passions, fixations and the like, the person simply will not reason well. When considering the practical syllogism and how, without the integral part of prudence of reason, one could not arrive at a proper conclusion, *i.e.*, knowledge of what to do, those who suffer from the vice of precipitation will find the reasoning process difficult, and they will often draw the wrong conclusions because their judgment is affected by their passions. This is precisely why a time that is tumultuous, not peaceful, should not be a time in which the church would engage in whole scale, liturgical changes. It would be likely the case that due to the passions of the tumultuous times, the decisions made, or the reasoning process in making the changes, would likely not arrive at the proper conclusion of the practical syllogism.

B. Inconsideration

In the decision making process, following the act of counsel, the intellect makes an act of judgment over which means is best. When the intellect is affected by passion, one does not consider the various means and tends to act hastily without consideration of what one is doing or is to do. Inconsideration, sometimes called thoughtlessness, is a defect of and is contrary to right judgment, which takes away synesis and gnome. In other words, the person is not able to discern matters in regard to whether they be according to the common law or are extraordinary. This could easily happen in a time when large numbers of liturgical changes are suggested to be made as a result of being immersed in a period of elation. In other words, the people of that time would likely jump to certain conclusions about what should and should not be in the liturgy, what would be considered legitimate liturgical principle when it is not, etc., and this could easily result in the pope making decisions about what to allow in the liturgy, and what not to allow in the liturgy, as a result of the elation or passions of the time. Practically speaking, it would mean that a pope would not take sufficient time for deliberation,[169] and would hurry along liturgical changes, which are precipitous. He would not take his time to sort out which is the best liturgical change, or whether liturgical change should be made at all, because of the fact that he is being prompted, or is being moved by the elation or the sentiments or spirit of the time.

Inconsideration causes one to lack caution and circumspection. Inconsideration rejects and neglects to attend to those things which proceed from right reason. Passion which causes inconsideration also destroys the ability of the intellect to know the particular as it pertains to or falls under the universal. It destroys one's ability to judge when a universal principle applies in a given set of circumstances. This is always the danger of living in a time which is prone to making decisions, based upon the passions, sentiments, emotions, and urges of the time. What is likely to happen is that authentic liturgical and Catholic principle will not be applied in the concrete, because the people will be seeking something to fulfill their passions, rather than what is best in relationship to the liturgy, *i.e.*, that which is likely to give the best form of worship to God.

C. Inconstancy

When someone suffers passion, he is unable to carry out the command of reason.[170] For example, in a time of war, a soldier may properly counsel and judge what should be done in a given battle and decide to do it, but then fear can take over and he does not command himself to do what he has chosen and thought should be done. This

---

[169] See Bouyer, *The Memoirs of Louis Bouyer*, p. 222, for a concrete example of liturgical proposals that lacked proper deliberation.

[170] Inconstancy is when one fails to command that which he has counseled and judged; see ST II-II, q. 53, a. 5.

defect is called inconstancy in that one commands something[171] but is unable to carry it out.[172] Often it indicates a commanding of something to be done at one moment, but then later changing one's mind or not carrying through due to the strength of the passion.[173] This defect indicates that one is unable to carry out universal precepts in the particular. Even if one reasons or counsels rightly and makes the right judgment about what to do, if the passion is strong, it can cause the intellect to be inconstant in its command about carrying out the chosen action. Often what occurs is that someone knows that something is good or bad, judging it rightly in a given situation, but is unable to carry out what is necessary to fulfill the precept regarding the good or bad action. This often leads to justification in which reason is weak in fulfilling the precept and so one seeks to exculpate himself, even to the point of rejecting the precept. Passion causes inconstancy because reason commands one thing, but then judges another, subsequent to the command. Since the passion is affecting the judgment, the intellect changes or is unable to carry out the original command.

St. Thomas says that one recedes from a prior proposed good because something disordered pleases him.[174] Since it pertains to reason to command, inconstancy is a defect of reason[175] and it pertains to imprudence.[176] Since it pertains to a defect of reason, inconstancy pertains to defects in some of the cognitive parts of prudence.

---

[171]This is why St. Thomas says it is contrary to the preceptive aspect of prudence; see ST II-II, q. 53, a. 2.

[172]St. Thomas notes that inconstancy implies a certain recession from an infinite proposed good; see ST II-II, q. 53, a. 5.

[173]ST II-II, q. 53, a. 5, ad 2.

[174]ST II-II, q. 53, a. 5.

[175]ST II-II, q. 53, a. 5.

[176]Ibid.

Inconstancy can arise due to improvidence,[177] *e.g.*, a young man gets the courage up to ask his girlfriend to marry him, but when he arrives to ask her, he finds that she is in a discussion with her parents who are insisting she not get married at this time. As a result, he backs away from asking her, because of fear of rejection due to the unforeseen circumstance of her parents discouraging her.

Inconstancy can arise out of a defect of understanding (*defectus intelligentiae*). Understanding is the integral part by which the person grasps the present situation, and if he fails to grasp it, he may not command something to be done because he will change his mind once he realizes that his counseled and chosen means will not work. Inconstancy can arise out of a defect of shrewdness (*solertia*). Sometimes the person is not quick enough to grasp the means which will really achieve the end, choosing instead a different means which later he recognizes will not work.

In the context of the liturgy all of this can apply, insofar as those in authority fail to enforce liturgical law. One of the admonitions that appears numerous times, as was noted, is that the priest does not have the authority to change the liturgy on his own. Moreover, the laity have a right to have the sacraments offered according to the rites of the Church,[178] but this was virtually never enforced. Neither the bishops nor the Vatican tend to enforce liturgical law, and it often appears either due to a desperation that the priests will not be obedient or out of human respect. In most cases, it is out of the latter. Yet, a pattern emerged during the 1900s where an innovation was introduced liturgically, even though it was contrary to liturgical law. It would spread into parts of the Church, and then the Vatican would

---

[177]The discussion of these defects can be seen in ST II-II, q. 53, a. 2. While the names of the defects are given here, the defects are opposed to the obvious integral parts as named above. These defects in relation to inconstancy also apply to the vice of negligence.

[178]CIC/83, c. 214.

allow it. This became the basis of many new liturgical practices, especially after the Second Vatican Council.

D. Negligence

Negligence is the last of the four species of imprudence and it implies a defect of due solicitude.[179] Negligence consists in a defect of an interior act which pertains to election[180] and the effect of negligence is omission.[181] Negligence occurs when someone does not choose to command an act which he should and so negligence, while pertaining to choice, is also about the act of commanding.[182] Negligence manifests a defect in which a person lacks a prompt will[183] to do what is right. Above, it was noted that the third opposite to the virtue of memory is the vice of negligence, which occurs when someone chooses not to remember, when he should do so. So negligence can include not only failing to command exterior acts, but also failing to command oneself to remember.

The negligence in policing the liturgical practices of priests is so ubiquitous as to not even need mentioning. However, it is brought up here to indicate that due to the lack of constancy and the negligence on the side of many in the Magisterium, it is simply not possible for an authentic liturgical development to arise out of these two vices. Often, the laity feel that they cannot find a Mass said properly, *i.e.*, according to the laws of the Church, virtually anywhere within a reasonable driving distance.

---

[179]ST II-II, q. 54, a. 1. In ibid., a. 2, St. Thomas says that negligence is opposed to solicitude.

[180]ST II-II, q. 54, a. 2.

[181]Ibid.

[182]Ibid.

[183]Ibid.

E. Carnal Prudence

Prudence is the virtue by which one commands a good means to a good end. But sometimes people enter into deliberation about means which are not morally good. Carnal prudence is a vice in which the good of the flesh is seen as the end of one's life,[184] and so one sets about deliberating on the means to satisfy the flesh. Carnal prudence disorders a man with respect to his final end;[185] for carnal prudence does not order man's actions to God, Who is man's true final end, but to some created good, more often than not, the good of the flesh.

> The flesh is for the sake of the soul as matter is for the sake of form and the instrument for the sake of the principal agent. And therefore one licitly loves the flesh as ordered toward the good of the soul as an end. If, however, the ultimate end is constituted in the very flesh, the love will be disordered and illicit. And in this way carnal prudence is ordered toward love of the flesh.[186]

One employs carnal prudence when he directs his means to the flesh as if it were the final end of his life, *i.e.*, if he thinks his happiness consists in the flesh or some created good. Prummer observes that carnal prudence is one in which "a suitable means is deliberated unto living according to the flesh or according to corrupt human nature, or

---

[184]ST II-II, q. 55, a. 1.

[185]Ibid.

[186]Ibid., ad 2: "Caro est propter anim am sicut materia propter formam et instrumentum propter principale agens. Et ideo sic licite diligitur caro ut ordinetur ad bonum animae sicut ad finem. Si autem in ipso bono carnis constituatur ultimus finis, erit inordinata et illicita dilectio. Et hoc modo ad amorem carnis ordinatur prudentia carnis."

even that which has the flesh as the ultimate end."[187] St. Paul observed that true prudence is subject to the law of God, whereas carnal prudence cannot please God,[188] because it employs immoral means to attain its end.

Here we begin to see a particular problem that has arisen among many bishops. They allow liturgical innovation or do things liturgically which has man as its focus. The very discussion of *ad orientem* as opposed to *versus populum*, is at the core of the discussion about whether the liturgy should conform itself to man (*i.e.*, the flesh) or to God. Will the liturgical action be done so as to face God or face the people? The same question would hold true in relation to any authentic liturgical development. Does the proposed liturgical change ultimately help human beings be more focused on God in their prayer and spiritual lives or does it draw one's focus on man. While it is true that the liturgy is an action which man performs and it is for his spiritual benefit, the primary end of the liturgy is to give God rightly ordered worship. In doing so, the secondary end of sanctifying man is most efficaciously achieved. However, when the liturgy becomes focused on man as its primary end or consideration, then the true primary end is mitigated, and even the secondary end of sanctifying man is diminished.

F. Craftiness (*Astutia*), Guile (*Dolus*) and Fraud (*Fraus*)

Craftiness, sometimes called cunning, slyness, or subtlety,[189] is the vice which inclines one to come to an end, either good or bad,

---

[187]Prummer, *Manuale Theologiae Moralis*, vol. 1, p. 461: "excogitat media idonea ad vivendum secundum carnem seu secundum corruptam naturam humanam, vel etiam quae habet bona carnis ut ultimatum finem vitae."

[188]Romans 8:6-8.

[189]Deferrari in *A Latin-English Dictionary of St. Thomas* (p. 97). The term "astuteness" in English is avoided, since in English this term normally has a positive connotation in which the person has an acute intelligence.

by not using true or good means, *i.e.*, means which are simulated[190] or apparent.[191] Craftiness is like solicitude because care is taken when considering the means but not in a true way.[192] Craftiness is executed through guile and fraud and is against the Christian virtue of simplicity.[193]

Guile is the vice by which craftiness is executed.[194] Deception is principally done by words and so guile is mostly attributed to speech[195] although it can also be by deeds. Guile is the vice in which the person is deceptive through words which are the means by which he achieves his end. The virtue of veracity[196] is essential for liturgical development, if for no other reason than that the goal is to reach the truth about the best form of liturgical worship, which has as its end God, Who is Truth Itself. It would not be possible to have a false means in the liturgy to achieve Truth Itself.

Fraud is the vice in which one is deceptive more by deeds than

---

[190]Simulation is the sin in which one does something in order to deceive someone else. Like lying which is the saying of the false in order to deceive (see ST II-II, q. 110), simulation is when one *does* (not necessarily says) something in order to deceive, *e.g.*, if someone asks a question and one gives a gesture which deceives the person, like pointing in the wrong direction or something of this sort, then one commits simulation. For a discussion of the sin of simulation, see ST II-II, q. 111.

[191]ST II-II, q. 55, a. 3; ibid., ad 2; and ST II-II, q. 111, q. 3, ad 2. Here the term apparent indicates that it is a means that appears good but is, in fact, morally bad.

[192]See ST II-II, q. 55, a. 3.

[193]Prummer, *Manuale Theologiae Moralis*, vol. 1, p. 461f.

[194]ST II-II, q. 55, a. 4.

[195]Ibid., ad 2.

[196]Regarding the nature of the virtue of veracity, see ST II-II, q. 109.

by words. The execution of *astutia* by deeds[197] is more proper to fraud than guile, which is by words and deeds but more principally words. The same observations apply to fraud as to guile.

It is here that a true honesty with ourselves is necessary regarding the architect of the liturgical changes that not only begot the *Novus Order Missae*, but also affected the traditional Latin Mass. Here, we consider the changes proposed from 1948 onward by Annibale Bugnini in which Fr. Louis Bouyer observed in his memoirs the methods of proposal by Bugnini. Essentially, Bugnini would devise changes he wanted in the liturgy and then tell the Concilium, or the various committees in the Concilium that were charged with proposing liturgical changes, that the pope wanted those particular changes. Bugnini would then go to the pope and tell the pope that the Concilium wanted the changes.[198] This was clearly fraud and deception, so much so that Fr. Bouyer, who is not prone to exaggeration, referred to Bugnini as a "mealy-mouthed scoundrel that the Neapolitan Vincentian, Bugnini, a man as bereft of culture as he was of basic honesty, soon revealed himself to be."[199] God does not work through fraud and deception and He will not reward those who do them or follow them. It is imprudent to implement liturgical changes made under such a set of circumstances.

V. Quodlibetals on Prudence in the Liturgy

There are several different aspects of prudence which come to bear on the question of liturgical change and development. One of these aspects is the question of frequency of change of the law.

---

[197]ST II-II, q. 55, a. 4. See also Prummer, *Manuale Theologiae Moralis*, vol. 1, p. 461f.

[198]Bouyer, *The Memoirs of Louis Bouyer*, p. 224f.

[199]Bouyer, *The Memoirs of Louis Bouyer*, p. 219. It should be observed that Bugnini himself admits to deceiving the pope on several occasions, which he testifies in his own book, *The Reform of the Liturgy*, passim.

Historically, the liturgical changes were done very gradually, over the course of time. Even when changes were made, the changes did not constitute some type of major alteration of liturgical practice. This is based on the principle formulated by St. Thomas:

> Hence, when the law is changed, the constraining power of the law is diminished, insofar as the custom is removed. And, therefore, the human law should never be changed, unless the common good is recompensed, to the degree that it is derogated.[200]

Since a change in the law diminishes the force of the law in the sense that the change goes contrary to what people were accustomed to do, unless the common good stands to benefit as much, if not more, from the change as the force of the law is diminished by the change, then the law should not be changed. Hence, the law, even liturgical law, would only be changed rarely, as well as not extensively.

Basic common observation of human behavior reveals that when the law is changed, it causes some lack of equilibrium for a time. In other words, it takes time for people to adjust to the new law and there is always a segment of the population that never really fully adjusts to the new law or a proper interpretation of the law. Furthermore, if too many laws are changed at once, the population goes through a period of confusion, and it often ends in some of the laws being followed and others ignored. In effect, the population can only psychologically absorb a certain amount of change in the law for the law to retain its force. If the laws are changed, not just in the number, but in frequency, this also has the same effect, but the psychology is somewhat different. If the law keeps changing, over the

---

[200]ST I-II, q. 97, a. 2: "unde quando mutatur lex, diminuitur vis constrictiva legis, inquantum tollitur consuetudo. et ideo nunquam debet mutari lex humana, nisi ex aliqua parte tantum recompensetur communi saluti, quantum ex ista parte derogatur."

course of time people stop observing the changes in the law, since human psychology is such that it takes energy to absorb a new law, and so people find it is too much energy to keep up with the law or they adopt the attitude of "why bother knowing the law since it is going to change soon anyway." Changing too many laws or changing the law too frequently results in an erosion of the force of the law in the minds of the people. They simply do not see the law as binding in the forum of conscience.

This appears to be what happened when the document *Sacrosanctum Concilium* introduced numerous areas of change in the liturgical law and practice; any cursory reading of the document bears this out. But after the document was issued and then a series of changes were made to the liturgy, and once the *Novus Order Missae* came out, the psychological status of the clergy was such that the law had lost a large part of is binding force. Obviously, priests of good will still tried to observe the laws of the Church regarding the liturgy, but then over the course of about 15 years after the *Novus Ordo* was promulgated, there were literally hundreds of documents and clarifications made on the liturgy. It was impossible for the clergy to keep up. This is added on top of the reality that the *Novus Ordo* itself allowed for many decisions about the liturgical practice within a given Mass, with all of the options that are part of the *General Instruction of the Roman Missal.*

Again, it is understandable why the Vatican kept repeating in its documentation from *Sacrosanctum Concilium* on, for about 10 years, that priests do not have the authority to change the liturgy on their own, because there was a clear grasp that the liturgy was being done in many places contrary to liturgical law or in a manner of the priest's own devising. It is still the case today, although it does seem to have improved in certain places. The point being is that it was imprudent to propose such wide sweeping liturgical changes since it was (a) contrary to how the Church had always done it in the past as a mere manner of prudence and Fear of the Lord, but also (b) because of their recognition that if there are too many changes, the liturgical law will lose its psychological force in the minds of the people and priests.[201]

Another principle that comes into play when assessing a liturgical change is the effect of the change, once made. Christ Himself enunciated the principle of judgment here, which is, "By their fruits you shall know them."[202] This is also based on the principle that the cause is always some way in the effect.[203] Once a liturgical change has occurred, the Magisterium has an obligation under prudence to practice solicitude in which they keep a watch over how things progress over the course of time regarding the liturgical change. Under normal circumstances, if the liturgical change was introduced observing all the principles that ought to govern liturgical change, there is likely not to be any harmful effects long term. However, if it is discovered that a liturgical change, or a set of liturgical changes, causes harm to the good of the Church, evidenced by drastic decline in Mass attendance, errors of faith in the people, decline of virtue in the clergy, etc., then those changes would have to be given serious consideration of nullifying. The Magisterium must have detachment from any changes made, so that an honest objective look could be given to the changes. Inability to admit error or that one is wrong regarding the liturgical changes proposed is a lack of humility.

Given all of the above, one particular consideration has to be given to the liturgical changes. Again, the Council of Trent observes:

> It declares furthermore, that in the dispensation of the sacraments, "salva illorum substantia", the Church may,

---

[201]The question is not one of legitimacy or of validity of liturgical reforms, as mentioned in the document *Traditiones Custodes*. The question is one of prudence and principle.

[202]Matthew 7:16.

[203]The principle is called the principle of resemblance, see Wuellner, *Summary of Scholastic Principles*, p. 97.

> according to circumstances, times and places, determine or change whatever she may judge most expedient for the benefit of those receiving them or for the veneration of the sacraments; and this power has always been hers.[204]

The Council is making it clear that the Church does have the authority to change the liturgy for the good of those who receive the sacraments. However, this does not mean that the liturgy should conform to the age. By that is meant that when making liturgical changes, one must take into consideration the Divine Positive Law and Natural Law, as well as human nature as laboring under the effects of original and actual sin, and not conform the liturgy to a particular age. In other words, an authentic liturgical change will be timeless, *i.e.*, even though it may address certain circumstances, it is normally going to be done in such a manner that it will perdure throughout time, because it will conform to a proper understanding of the unchanging human nature and Deposit of Faith.

As a matter of prudence, all liturgical changes would be bound to conform to all first principles, whether they be ontological, moral, or logical. For example, as a matter of prudence, the liturgy should not contain anything that is contradictory in itself, *i.e.*, among the various parts of the liturgy, nor contradicts the Deposit of Faith. Any violation of the first principles, as a matter of prudence, would result in the liturgical change eventually not being adopted, since it would be irrational and contrary to common sense.

One moral principle in particular, which has come up obliquely during this discussion of prudence, is the moral principle of doubt of fact. This principle has the following formulation: "when in doubt of

---

[204]Council of Trent, Session 21, c. 2: "Praeterea declarat hanc potestatem perpetuo in Ecclesia fuisse ut in sacramentorum dispensatione salva illorum substantia ea statueret vel mutaret quae suscipientium utilitati seu ipsorum sacramentorum venerationi pro rerum temporum et locorum varietate magis expedire iudicaret."

fact, do not act." This is known by anyone who has use of reason, and is exemplified by the example of the moving bush. If a hunter is out hunting deer and he sees a bush rustling, he does not simply stick his gun in the bush and pull the trigger. The rustling may or may not be caused by a deer (doubt of fact). Rather, if it turns out that it was a human being rustling in the bush, he would have just shot a human being (hence, do not act). People have a moral obligation under prudence to know the circumstances sufficiently well in order to be able to act. When the circumstances are not known sufficiently well, one must not act, but take means to secure sufficient knowledge of the circumstances.

Above, it was discussed that the liturgical movement was in its nascent stage in the 1940s and 1950s. There simply had not been enough research done to begin the process of making liturgical changes. Subsequent studies have shown that many of the conclusions about the nature of the liturgical activities in the early Church have proven to be inaccurate. Moreover, many of the aspects of the liturgy are shrouded in antiquity and are not known as to their source (possible Apostolocity), hence, without a clear knowledge of the source, one ought not change it until the source can be clearly determined.[205]

Furthermore, prudence also deals with the circumstance of why (*cur*) and when looking at the liturgical changes, it is often presumed that if one can determine the history of the liturgical change, and those historical circumstances no longer apply, then one can make the liturgical change to that element. However, the historical facts around the case do not necessarily touch upon the *why* a liturgical

---

[205]Kwasniewski, *True Obedience*, p. 85, footnote 41: "It is important to note here that, when it comes to the oldest elements of liturgical rites, we often have no way of knowing and may never have the ability to know, which of these are of merely ecclesiastical institution and which are of divine, apostolic, or subapostolic institution, which makes it all the more crucial not to eliminate any of them."

development occurred. That is to say, there are liturgical changes that were introduced based upon human reason enlightened by faith, but sometimes God moves the human agent to do something without the human agent having full knowledge of the why of it. This applies to many liturgical elements that were organically developed and have been in the liturgy for centuries: even though we may know *when* they were introduced, that does not give us the full picture of *why* God had them introduced. This is why the principle of the longer something is in the liturgy, the more it is the Will of God is important. Often, it is upon reflection of the longevity of the element in the liturgy which gives us a sense of why God had it there in the first place.

Conclusion

At times, when liturgical elements are discussed in regard to the possibility of changing them, we often hear it is a matter of prudence. However, as shown above, imprudence in its various forms is sinful, so the import of something being imprudent is not just a matter of it not turning out well or for the best. It can be a matter of acting contrary to reason or the faith. It is necessary that when the limits of papal authority over the liturgy are considered, due to the Divine Positive Law and the Natural Law, it is outside of his authority to knowingly act contrary to prudence. This is not a matter of *should* not, but a matter of *ought* not act contrary to prudence.

Clearly, there are times when a course of action regarding the liturgy seems prudent, even eliminating as much lack of certitude regarding the change as possible, and that a pope acts upon propositions or suggestions. However, since historically the changes were only made when necessary to maximize prudence and to avoid offending God and causing a disturbance in the minds of the faithful, the pope would still have to take due diligence when making any changes. As a general rule, changes would only be made when there is a proportionate grave cause, since danger of lessening the binding force of the liturgical law in the minds of the faithful would be diminished and the possibility of offending God would be entirely eliminated. Augmentation or new additions to the liturgy would be governed by slightly different principles, while still maintaining the principles so far discussed. Nevertheless, even new additions, other than augmentation or additions to the liturgical calendar, would normally be done only when necessary and rarely as a matter of the virtue of caution in order to avoid the liturgical law being diminished in the minds of the priests and faithful.

Chapter VI: A Few Particular Liturgical Matters

I. Observations on the Principle of Evidence

One of the areas that has affected virtually every single science in modern times revolves around the application of the principle of evidence. In some modern empirical scientists' beliefs, evidence can simply be dismissed, if it does not fit their hypothesis. This practice has been evident in the Church as well, and most likely, it is a particular problem with modernism itself, since the principle of immanence does not have to admit of objective evidence for its conclusions. Nevertheless, it would behoove the discussion to address the principle of evidence and how it should be applied in liturgical studies.

A. First Principles

In order to really see how the principle of evidence itself applies, a short discursus on first principles is necessary.[1] First principles are studied in first philosophy which is a branch of metaphysics.[2] As with any philosophical consideration, it is necessary to discuss the definition of certain concepts before one can proceed. The definition of a principle is as follows:

> **Principle, n. 1.** That from which something in some way follows; a being or truth from which being, change, knowledge, or discussion, respectively, starts. **2.** Any cause. (For cause is the main type of principle.) **3.** Anything that is in any way first even if it has no connection with later members.[3]

---

[1]This section is taken in substance from Ripperger, *The Metaphysics of Evolution*, p. 7-14.

[2]See Thomas Aquinas, *In Duodecim Libros Metaphysicorum Aristotelis Expositio*, proemium.

[3]Wuellner, *A Dictionary of Scholastic Philosophy*, p. 244.

There are different kinds of principles given the definition. There are some principles which follow from other principles but those principles, which are first, are those which do not come from another principle and which have no prior principles in their own series.[4] To have no prior principles in its own series means that in that category of first principles, there are no other principles prior to that principle.

Some principles relate to being itself, *i.e.,* to real things, while others determine how we know a thing or come to knowledge of a thing. In the order of being, there is what is called a:

> **real** principle, the principle from which being proceeds; a being from which another being or modification of being proceeds in some way. Real principles include beginning, foundation, origin, location, condition, cause of any type, and elements of composition.[5]

Real principles tell us something about the very nature of being. Real principles are counter distinguished from logical or what are sometimes called gnoseological principles.

> **Logical principle:** (1) a principle of knowledge; a truth from which other truth proceeds; a source of knowledge or a cause of thought. These include definitions, signs, questions, problems, sources of truth, axioms, norms, premises, bases of division, etc. (2) a rule of logic. (3) a methodological principle or rule of procedure special to a science.[6]

---

[4]Ibid.

[5]Ibid., p. 245.

[6]Ibid., p. 244. A formal principle is one of the basic principles and rules to justify the validity of reasoning, such as the principle of non-contradiction. All formal principles are logical principles, but not all logical principles are formal principles. This is due to the fact that a logical principle deals with knowledge in

A logical principle is one that governs how we come to know a thing, and logical principles are said to be built into the very structure of our intellect. By virtue of the fact that they are built into our intellect by nature, they are said to be connatural. Something is connatural which belongs "to a nature and exist[s] in it from its beginning; congenital or innate; not acquired; present in and operating by natural endowment, tendency or need of nature."[7] Something is connatural which is in the very nature of the thing; it is innate or possessed from the very beginning and it is not acquired or added.[8] It is connatural to the human intellect to perform its operations according to the first principles, *e.g.*, it is contrary to the nature of the intellect to violate the principle of non-contradiction. In the writings of St. Thomas, we see that there are natural habits regarding the first principles of the intellect. These habits are connatural or natural in the sense that they are not acquired, but are in the intellect from the beginning. St. Thomas discusses what he calls the natural habit[9] of *intellectus principiorum* or understanding of the [first] principles. It is a natural or innate[10] habit by which we are able to understand the first principles, and insofar as it is innate, it is found equally in all men.[11] This habit helps one to grasp or understand those first principles

---

general, whereas formal principles deal with the principles governing logic or reasoning.

[7]Ibid., p. 59.

[8]Sometimes acquired habits and virtues are said to be connatural, as if to indicate that they constitute a second nature. However, they are not connatural in the proper sense, since they are not innate.

[9]See III Sent., d. 23, q. 3, a. 2, ad 1; ST I, q. 58, a. 3; ibid., q. 79, a. 12; ST I-II, q. 51, a. 1 and ibid., q. 57, a. 2 and De Ver., q. 1, a. 12.

[10]II Sent., d. 24, q. 2, a. 3.

[11]ST II-II, q. 5, a. 4, ad 3.

without inquisition or motion of the intellect,[12] *i.e.*, once the terms are grasped and the formulation of the first principle is heard or thought, one immediately knows or understands the meaning and truth of the principle. This natural habit moves the intellect to grasp the first principles immediately, without ratiocination. This means that one does not grasp the first principles as in a conclusion,[13] but they are grasped immediately as self-evident.[14]

Since they are self-evident, one must give assent to the first principles[15] as moved by this natural habit. Moreover, it means that one cannot err regarding the first principles,[16] *i.e.,* reason is always right when it grasps the first principles. However, the history of philosophy, the history of man, as well as common sense experience have shown that man does not always act according to these principles or he does not understand them. Some philosophers have denied

---

[12]II Sent., d. 3, q. 1, a. 6, ad 2; ibid., d. 24, q. 3, a. 3, ad 2; III Sent., d. 27, q. 1, a. 3, ad 1 and *De malo* q. 16, a. 5.

[13]ST I-II, q. 65, a. 1, ad 3. This would indicate that the Cartesian mentality that one must be able to prove something for it to be true cannot stand for two reasons. The first is that the first principles from which all other conclusions are drawn are self-evident, *i.e.*, grasped immediately without proof. One can only show that, if one rejects a first principle, one is left in absurdity. The second is if everything must be proven, the first principles must be proven by syllogistic reasoning and the premises of that syllogism must be proven, etc., *ad infinitum*. The problem is that there would never be a first principle and subsequently never anything after it. The impossibility of an infinite regress regarding principles militates against the Cartesian notion of everything having to be proven. This would apply equally to the empirical sciences as well as to all the other sciences.

[14]I Sent., d. 3, q. 1, a. 4, ad 3; ST I, q. 17, a. 3, ad 2; SCG II, c. 47, n. 3 and De Ver., q. 10, a. 11, ad 12.

[15]ST I, q. 82, a. 2. See also De Ver., q. 15, a. 1.

[16]ST I, q. 17, a. 3, ad 2.

implicitly the first principles of the speculative intellect in their philosophical discourses.[17] However, there are two reasons why first principles are repudiated. The first is that the person does not understand the terms of the principle, and therefore, cannot give assent to it because he cannot understand the formulation of the principle since it is composed of terms not understood. The second is that there is something impeding the use of reason. For example, the young cannot make use of the habit,[18] because they have not reached sufficient maturity to think abstractly enough to grasp the principles fully. The gravely mentally ill cannot make use of the habit, because of reason's inability to function properly. In fact, one of the ways we know someone is mentally ill is by virtue of the fact that they do not act according to first principles, *e.g.*, they contradict themselves or assert things which violate the principle of sufficient reason. Another impediment is the foolishness of the person, *i.e.*, as Aristotle observes, it pertains to the fool to deny what is self-evident; or we may say a person who denies self-evident principles is irrational.

This is an important point in the context of liturgical discussions. At times, there is an attitude among certain members of the Magisterium, but also among many theologians in the past 70 years, that first principles can just be ignored when discussing matters that pertain to theology or even liturgical matters. The laity have the Natural Law built into their intellects, and so any liturgical activity that does not line out with first principles is going to slowly be rejected by them. Furthermore, any discussion of the liturgy, if it is true, must adhere to the first principles.

---

[17]For example, Hume in his critique of causality not only denies the principle of causality, which is self-evident, but he must also deny the principle of sufficient reason and non-contradiction as a result of his rejection of the principle of causality. Hegel, in his dialectic, holds that in the synthesis both contradictories are contained in the synthesis together, thereby indicating that reason gives assent to two things which are contradictory.

[18]ST I-II, q. 94, a. 1, ad 4.

B. The Principle of Evidence

One of the first principles is the principle of evidence, and it is necessary to consider two aspects of the principle, *viz.*, the principle itself and then its application in liturgical discussions. The principle of evidence is based upon the principle of sufficient reason,[19] but has a slightly different formulation: "*The Principle of Sufficient Reason*, logical formula: Every judgment (affirmative or negative) about a being should have a sufficient reason (that is, sufficient evidence)."[20] The full formula of the principle of evidence is: "The objective evidence of being is the criterion of the truth of assent and the motive for certain assent."[21] Another formulation of it is: "The thing in the condition of evidence is the measure of the truth of judgments."[22] Essentially this means that objective reality of the thing constitutes the measure and standard of the truth of our judgments.

By way of initial observations, what this essentially means in the context of liturgical research and science is that any statement about a liturgical act, practice, phrase, etc., must be based in sufficient evidence. One practice that is done by some clergy and "experts" in liturgical discussions is asserting things that have no basis in reason or in fact, *e.g.*, asserting that certain liturgical practices occurred in the early Church, when the evidence is to the contrary. A concrete example of this would be that after studying free-standing altars in early churches, liturgists in the 1930s concluded that priests once

---

[19]Wuellner lists the principle of evidence in the section on the principle of sufficient reason, among other places, see *Summary of Scholastic Principles*, p. 15f, princ. 35. The principle of sufficient reason is: "There is a sufficient reason or adequate necessary objective explanation for the being of whatever is and for all attributes of any being."

[20]Ibid.

[21]Ibid., p. 43, princ. 155.

[22]Ibid.

celebrated Mass "facing the people," and that it was only because of clericalism in medieval ages that the priests turned their backs on the people. There was simply no evidence for such an assertion, and so that proposition violates the principle of evidence. In this respect, if the pope is going to introduce a liturgical practice *based on the tradition*, he needs to make sure there is sufficient evidence for it in the tradition.[23]

The principle of evidence also has some corollaries, which are highly important in parsing out. One corollary, which we see violated frequently in modern scientific studies, but it was also evidenced and continues to be evident among certain writers in the area of the liturgy, is the following: "No argument or conclusion contrary to evident facts is valid."[24] This corollary is sometimes reformulated as "An hypothesis or explanation which contradicts evident facts is not rationally tenable."[25] Sometimes this is formulated as: "a single piece of evidence contrary to a hypothesis or conclusion invalidates the hypothesis or conclusion, either in part or in whole," or "no inference contrary to the fact(s) is true," and "There is no argument against the evidence."[26]

Often what happens in the context of liturgical discussions is that certain Fathers or authors are simply dismissed, because what they say does not line out with the modernist inclinations regarding what is wanted in the liturgy. It is for this reason that we must follow the principle: when in doubt, favor goes to the tradition. This is due to the fact that any discussion about what happened has to come from

---

[23]A corollary to the principle of evidence is: "Every judgment must be based on evidence, but self-evident judgments do not need demonstration." (Ibid., p. 63, princ. 288).

[24]Ibid., princ. 289.

[25]Ibid., princ. 290.

[26]Ibid., princ. 156.

the tradition itself, the monuments, etc. But also, the tradition seems to be proven true repeatedly, even in some of the aspects of the tradition that enjoy the lowest theological note. However, the point in all of this is that any legitimate liturgical discussion has to take into account *all* of the evidence, which ultimately comes to us via the tradition.[27] Any single piece of evidence contrary to any liturgical theory invalidates the theory in part or in whole. The advancement of the science of theology in the area of liturgical studies *must* adhere to this principle, if there is to be any semblance of honesty in the endeavor, as well as any real advancement in the science. When one listens to various liturgical "experts," often things will be asserted that have no basis in fact, which is contrary to the principle of evidence. This is one of the reasons that this author appears to have observed a growing intellectual frustration with many theologians and Magisterial members in the Church, because there is a systematic denial of the liturgical realities today as well as a systemic ignoring of the facts of the tradition.

Also, we continue to encounter assertions about what God wants in the liturgy, divorced from Apostolicity, longevity, prudence, or any other aspect of the tradition. Yet, this is based on the proper logical response in relation to gratuitous assertions, *viz.*, what is gratuitously asserted can be gratuitously denied. As theologians in the last 70 years or so began asserting what was and what is part of liturgical tradition and history without any foundation, as well as what the significance of certain liturgical actions were, these assertions had no basis in Catholic tradition or theology. These began to be implemented, only to cause intellectual dissonance in the minds of the Catholics who know their faith well. It is for this reason, for any liturgical change to appeal to the faithful, or one may even say for the liturgy to appeal to a faithful Catholic, it must have three things as part of it, otherwise the liturgical practice asserted will cause a slow

---

[27]This is based on the principle that (ibid., princ. 157): "an explanation or hypothesis must take into account *all* the evidence." (Emphasis his).

disintegration in the life of the Church: (1) the liturgy must appeal to reason,[28] (2) be illumined by faith,[29] and (3) based in fact (tradition and reality).[30] This last criteria is important, because the principle of the criterion of truth, which states that "Things (forms) are the measure of the truth of the human mind,"[31] is not what we want to believe that is the criteria for truth, especially in the liturgy, but what is the objective reality, which is known via the tradition.

Above all, we are left with the reality that "the divine intellect is the measure of the truth of all things."[32] Throughout this book, we have discussed the various ways in which the mind of God can be known regarding the elements of the liturgy. However, the fact that modernists want to make the human mind (principle of immanence) the standard of truth rather than God, ultimately, constitutes the fundamental reason why the direction they push liturgical changes is almost always away from God. This is evident in the debate over *ad orientem* and *versus populum*, the conforming of liturgical language

---

[28]Anything contrary to reason or unreasonable will be rejected by the faithful over the course of time. In liturgical discussions, one cannot ignore liturgical texts from the past to assert what one thinks is the case historically, etc. Some modern Magisterial members act like the last 70 years of liturgical changes are well grounded, despite being divorced from the evidence in the tradition or even being ignorant of tradition (not much evidence was known and is only now becoming known), they assert things of the tradition that are contrary to the evidence or do not have sufficient degree of certitude.

[29]It must adhere to authentic Catholic teaching as relating to the Deposit of Faith, which is the rule of faith.

[30]The principle of evidence must be able to be shown as operative. Sheer fiat on the side of one in authority may result in immediate obedience and compliance, but will result in deterioration of that obedience over the course of time.

[31]Ibid., p. 107, princ. 530.

[32]Ibid., princ. 525.

to modern errors or forms of expression, rather than as the saints formulated them thoughout history, and the concern about offending people over the possible offense to God that a particular liturgical practice might involve.

One of the criteria that is being ignored is the fruits to the liturgical changes. Heretics will ignore any decline in the attendance, fervor, devotion and, ultimately, even the participation of the numbers of faithful in order to maintain a theological position which is contrary to the Will of God. Christ said, "you will know them by their fruits."[33] However, any discussion of the reality that the Church has declined in every category of metric,[34] except conversions in Africa, and its possible connection to liturgical changes is *a priori* seen as touching on schismatic or heretical thinking. The liturgical changes in the last 70 years are not open to discussion and any discussion of them is seen as negative, overly critical, suspect, and disobedient. The problem is that this mindset flies in the face of the principle of evidence. Basic human intellectual inquiry into the causes of things seeks to identify the evidence and analyzes it scientifically and precisely without agenda or emotional bias. To deny the faithful the intellectual endeavor to begin discovery of the root of the problem is itself to perpetuate the problem. We are obviously living in a time of bad fruit in the Church and any reasonable person would be open to finding the true source of the problem, regardless of how painful it might be personally. That also means that we must take a serious look at the liturgical changes to see which, if any of them, led to specific areas of decline in Church life.

The second thing of importance regarding the principle of evidence has to do with the question of certitude. Again, the principle states: "The objective evidence of being is the criterion of the truth of

---

[33]Matthew 7:16. Interesting that Matthew 7:15 makes references to false prophets.

[34]Jones, *Index of Leading Catholic Indicators*, passim.

assent and the motive for certain assent."[35] The certitude of a proposition is based upon the evidence itself. So if the evidence is such that there is absolutely no ability to deny it and that the evidence is without doubt to the human mind, then one has a high degree of certitude about the truth of the proposition. However, because of the limitations of the human intellect, in relation to certain matters, the evidence simply is not enough to have a high degree of certitude. In fact, the degree of certitude is based upon the certainty of the evidence itself. This is obviously the foundation for the varying theological notes. The application in the area of liturgical studies is also key and requires, therefore, two reasonable approaches. The first is a matter of knowledge, *viz.*, there are going to be things in the tradition regarding the liturgy which will be of varying theological note, and therefore, will have varying degrees of certitude. While most humans would find it enjoyable to have high degrees of certitude in all areas, that simply is not the reality in which we operate due to lack of numbers of sources regarding a particular thing (such as only one Father as opposed to numerous Fathers upholding some liturgical practice) or that the sources we do have do not admit by their very nature of certitude about the truth of the proposition.[36]

The second reasonable approach regarding the degrees of certitude based upon the evidence in liturgical studies is how to prudentially proceed. We have discussed this already, but attention should be drawn to the fact that many assertions about liturgical elements made in the last 70 years or so had very little or no foundation in the evidence. Yet, certain members of the Church proceeded as if the level of certitude was high, when the evidence did not admit it; thereby violating the principle of evidence. Conversely, when there is not sufficient evidence, then the most prudent thing is

---

[35]Ibid., p. 43, princ. 155.

[36]An example of this would be St. Thomas' discussion of the *Mysterium Fidei*. See below.

to leave that element alone without change, unless there is grave cause. Again, it is analogous to opening the hood of a car and not knowing what all of the wires are for. While the fact might be clear as to exactly what a particular wire does, due to human limitations, we may not know what the wire does. Therefore, to remove it or modify it without knowing what it does runs the danger of causing serious problems in the running of the engine of the car. In like manner, when it comes to the liturgy, if the evidence is not clear or lacks a high degree of theological note, then reasonableness or prudence dictates *not* changing that element or thinking it is open to change, but caution in leaving it until sufficient solid evidence arises about its nature. This all being said, there are a few particular elements that demonstrate these varying degrees of certitude, and therefore, will have an impact on the nature of the authority the pope may have over the element as well as prudentially how he may be morally bound to proceed.

II. Exactitude of Worship, Again

We had already seen that God in the Old Testament and the New Testament, as well as the Church's practice throughout history, has been one in which there is precision in how we are to worship God. We quote, again, Pope Pius XII in this regard:

> Thus we observe that when God institutes the Old Law, He makes provision besides for sacred rites, and determines in exact detail the rules to be observed by His people in rendering Him the worship He ordains. To this end He established various kinds of sacrifice and designated the ceremonies with which they were to be offered to Him. His enactments on all matters relating to the Ark of the Covenant, the Temple and the holy days are minute and clear. He established a sacerdotal tribe with its high priest, selected and described the vestments with which the sacred ministers were to be clothed, and every function in any way pertaining to divine worship. Yet this was nothing more than a faint

> foreshadowing of the worship which the High Priest of the New Testament was to render to the Father in heaven.[37]

This section of *Mediator Dei* was quoted in relation to the fact that God revealed precisely how He was to be worshiped. This constitutes a general principle, *viz.*, that we as creatures are obligated to worship God in a due mode (the virtue of religion under the justice) as determined *by Him*. In effect, it requires the creature to obey God, when He has revealed how worship is to be done as part of the Natural Law.[38] While this is also part of the Divine Positive Law, Pius XII is noting above that there are specifics that God has given. It is not just a general principle, but the general principle is applied based upon what we know from the Divine Positive Law (*i.e.*, Revelation). We are bound to the particulars of worship determined by God. These particulars are found not just in Revelation, but even as was shown in Apostolic tradition and by God revealing His will to us about what He wants in the liturgy based upon the principle of longevity. Some of the particulars have already been discussed above as seen in divine or divino-Apostolic tradition, such as the words of Consecration, and the general flow of the Mass including an Offertory, Consecration and Holy Communion. These have high degrees of theological note. Yet, there are other particulars

---

[37]Pius XII, *Mediator Dei*, para.16: "Itaque, si Deum consideramus veterem condentem legem, eum cernimus de sacris etiam ritibus edere praecepta, accuratasque decernere normas, quibus populus obtemperet in legitimo eidem praestando cultu. Quamobrem varia statuit sacrificia, variasque designavit caerimonias, quibus dicatum sibi munus offerretur; eaque omnia perspicue significavit, quae ad foederis arcam, ad templum, ad diesque festos pertinerent. Sacerdotalem tribum et summum sacerdotem constituit; ac vestes etiam indicavit ac descripsit, quibus sacrorum administri uterentur, et quidquid aliud praeterea ad divinum cultum respiceret."

[38]That God is to be obeyed is part of the third category of natural inclination of the Natural Law.

that have been noted through the history of the Church, and so a few of those will be discussed here. It is not the intention of this author, nor the scope of the book, to address all of the particulars that can be traced in some manner to the Will of God in the various ways already discussed. Rather, it is to provide a few examples, so that a proper set of conclusions can be drawn.

III. Some Particulars

A. Substance of the Sacraments

We have already seen that the Council of Trent has noted that the Church does not have authority over the substance of the sacraments. In relation to the Eucharist, the Church does not have authority to change the essential form of "This is My Body" and "This is the chalice[39] of My Blood."[40] This would also include not having the authority to promulgate a rite which did not contain the essential form, as was noted, due to the nature of the words not having the *vis sacramentis*. Nor would the Church have the authority to determine the matter of this sacrament.[41] For example, the Church, and therefore, the pope would not have the right to change the matter from bread to potato chips. Yet, he would have the authority of preservation, insofar as he would have the right to enforce in the confecting of this sacrament by the priests that they use the proper matter and form. The pope would also have the right, as the "custodian of the mysteries of God,"[42] *i.e.*, the protector of the integrity of the elements of sanctification, to sanction any priest

---

[39]Regarding the word "chalice" as part of the form, see ST III, q. 78, a. 3, ad 1.

[40]ST III, q. 78.

[41]See ST III, q. 74. See also Francisco Suarez, *De sacramentis*, disp. XV, sect. iii (Comm. in IIIam D. Thomae, tom. III).

[42]I Cor. 4:1.

should he attempt to confect the Eucharist not using the proper matter and form.

B. Mixing Water in the Wine

Suarez notes that:

> Therefore I say firstly, that the Sacramental ceremonies, which are beside [*extra*] the substance of the sacraments, although they [the ceremonies] have been introduced at different times in imitation of or after the example of Christ, yet are not immediately instituted by Him. The first part is clear, partly from what has been said in the preceding section; and partly again it can readily be shown by examples: for in confecting the Eucharist, there came from the example of Christ the mixing of water with wine, as Cyprian testifies.[43]

Gihr gives a further explanation:

> It is certain that the Lord at the institution of the Eucharist consecrated wine mixed with water, since the addition of water to the wine at the paschal meal was a permanent and universally practiced custom from which the Lord surely did not depart. The ancient liturgies and holy Fathers are unanimous in asserting that the Saviour mixed water with the wine at the Last Supper. Thus from the time of the apostles the Church has everywhere and at all times faithfully followed the example of her divine Master and has ever consecrated only wine mixed with water. She regarded it, as St. Cyprian writes in his letter to Caecilius, as proper that at the mixing and offering of the chalice of the Lord, she should observe the true tradition, so that at His glorious and triumphant return He may find us adhering strictly to that which He had exhorted

---

[43]Suarez, *loc. cit.*

> us, observing what He had taught and doing what He had done.[44]

While the mixing of the water and the wine do not touch upon the validity of the sacrament, if it is not done,[45] nevertheless, it did come from Christ through the Apostles and was maintained as a universal practice of the Church *ab initio*, and is not merely a matter of ecclesiastical precept, since it came from the Apostles.[46] Even the Council of Trent mentions that it is believed that Christ the Lord did this.[47] This particular element of the liturgy would then be outside the scope of the pope to change, since it has the quality of Apostolicity, despite it not affecting validity, if not done.

C. The *Mysterium Fidei*

The next particular element has to do with the insertion of the *Mysterium Fidei* into the words of Consecration. One of the primary sources for this discussion is from St. Thomas Aquinas. In his *Summa Theologiae*, he noted that:

> The Evangelists did not intend to give the forms of the sacraments, which were necessary to hide in the early Church,

---

[44]Gihr, *The Holy Sacrifice of the Mass*, p. 548f.

[45]ST III, q. 74, a. 7. See also Gihr, *loc. cit.*

[46]Gihr observes in *ibid.,* footnote 28: "The mingling of the wine with water is not *de necessitate sacramenti neque praecepti divini*, but only *de necessitate praecepti ecclesiastici*, that is, *apostolici*. In the Fathers and in councils and liturgies, the Eucharistic chalice, that is, its contents (before the Consecration), has, for example, the following denominations: крао, крана тотпрк кекрадіно, calix mixtus, temperamentum calicis, poculum aquae et vini, calix dominicus vino mixtus, calix vini et aquae plenus, vinum aqua mixtum, calix dominicus vino et aqua permixtus."

[47]Council of Trent, sess. XXII, c. 7 and can. 9.

> as Dionysius says, at the end of the *Ecclesiastical Hierarchy*. But they did intend to reveal the history of Christ. And nevertheless, all of the words are able to be born from the diverse places of Scripture. For which He said, "This is the chalice," is had in Luke 22 and I Cor. 11. In Matthew, moreover, is said, "This is My Blood of the New Testament, which for many will be poured out in remission of sins." To which, however, is added, "eternal" and again, "the Mystery of Faith," is had from the tradition of Our Lord, which comes to the Church through the Apostles, according to I Cor. 11, "I have accepted from the Lord that which also I gave unto you."[48]

This passage from St. Thomas is interesting, since it contains a few things which may escape the reader, if he is not paying close attention. First, is that St. Thomas is saying that the full formula of the words of Consecration in the tradition were not given in Scripture all together,

---

[48]ST III, q. 78, a. 3, ad 9: "evangelistae non intendebant tradere formas sacramentorum, quas in primitiva ecclesia oportebat esse occultas, ut dicit Dionysius, in fine ecclesiasticae hierarchiae. Sed intenderunt historiam de christo texere. Et tamen omnia haec verba fere ex diversis scripturae locis accipi possunt. Nam quod dicitur, Hic est Calix, habetur Luc. xxii et I Cor. xi. Matthaei autem xxvi dicitur, Hic est Sanguis Meus Novi Testamenti, qui pro multis effundetur in remissionem peccatorum. Quod autem additur, aeterni, et iterum, Mysterium Fidei, ex traditione Domini habetur, quae ad ecclesiam per apostolos pervenit, secundum illud I Cor. xi, ego accepi a domino quod et tradidi vobis." In IV Sent., d. 8, q. 2, a. 2a, ad 1, St. Thomas says essentially the same thing: "verba supradicta ex magna parte possunt ex diversis locis sacrae scripturae colligi, quamvis non inveniantur alicubi simul scripta. Quod enim dicitur: hic est calix, habetur Luc. 22, et 1 Corinth. 2. Quod autem dicitur: novi testamenti, ex tribus habetur, Matth. 26, et Marc. 14, et Luc. 22. Quod autem dicitur, aeterni, et iterum, mysterium fidei, ex traditione Domini habetur, quae per apostolos ad ecclesiam pervenit, secundum illud 1 Corinth. 11, 23: ego enim accepi a domino quod et tradidi vobis. Evangelistae enim non intendebant formas et ritus sacramentorum tradere, sed dicta et facta Domini enarrare."

since the evangelists were not intending to give the exact forms of the sacraments. Obviously, they do recount the essential words of some of the forms.

Second, St. Thomas then observes that the various words that are part of the full form of Consecration of the Precious Blood do find themselves in Scripture, specifically 1 Timothy 3:9. The phrase *Mysterium Fidei* appears in the context of referring to the qualifications of a man who is to become a deacon, *viz.*, that he is to hold to "the mystery of faith in a pure conscience."[49] Essentially, St. Paul appears to be saying the deacon has to believe in the Eucharist as the Real Presence (the very meaning of *Mysterium Fidei*, as the Eucharist is THE mystery of faith), in a clear conscience. St. Thomas says that this clear conscience ultimately means that one is without error regarding the faith.[50]

Third, St. Thomas goes on to assert that "'the Mystery of Faith' is had from the tradition of Our Lord, which comes to the Church through the Apostles, according to I Cor. 11, 'I have accepted from the Lord that which also I gave unto you.'" There are three things in this short passage. The first is that St. Thomas is asserting that the *Mysterium Fidei* comes from Our Lord. Yet, what is not clear is in what manner. Did Our Lord use those words during the Last Supper? None of the Gospel accounts give that testimony, but St.Thomas says that the evangelists were not giving exact forms. Yet, if it came from Our Lord, was it something He mentioned in the instruction of the Apostles as to the nature of the Eucharist? Lastly, was it something that Christ *post resurrectionem* commanded the Apostles to insert into the words of Consecration? St. Thomas just indicates that it comes to us from Our Lord through the Apostles. Given this, it would not appear that the theological note of this is very high.

---

[49]The Latin is: "habentes mysterium fidei in conscientia pura."

[50]Ad I Tim., 3, c. 3, l. 2.

Nicholas Gihr simply states what is the common opinion on the matter, *viz.*, "Christ's sacrificial Blood in the chalice is a mystery of faith in the fullest sense of the term."[51] Fiedrowicz, after noting what Gihr noted, states that:

> In the period in which this extension of the second consecration formula occurred (fourth/seventh century), the *mysterium fidei* would have been primarily a proclamation – originally perhaps completed by the deacon – of the soteriological significance of the chalice.[52]

This obviously became the practice as of late. However, Jungmann tends to dispute this claim:

> And then, in the middle of the sacred text, stand the enigmatic words so frequently discussed: *mysterium fidei*. Unfortunately, the popular explanation (that the words were originally spoken by the deacon to reveal to the congregation what had been performed at the altar, which was screened from view by curtains) is poetry, and not history.[53]

Jungmann then footnotes what appears to be the historical genesis of this explanation, which appears to be a much later explanation than what is in the tradition. Jungmann continues: "The phrase is found inserted in the earliest texts of the sacramentaries, and mentioned even

---

[51]Gihr, *Holy Sacrifice of the Mass*, p. 641. Gihr refers the reader to St. Thomas' passage noted above in the *Tertia Pars* of the *Summa Theologiae* for reference.

[52]Fiedrowicz, *The Traditional Mass*, p. 280.

[53]Jungmann, *The Mass of the Roman Rite*, vol. 2, p. 199.

in the seventh century. It is missing only in some later sources."[54] Jungmann ultimately holds that the exact time and reason for insertion is not clear.[55] However, for him, what is clear is that it comes from Roman origin.[56] He goes on to uphold the common interpretation, *viz.*, "The chalice of the New Testament is the life giving symbol of truth, the sanctuary of our belief."

Jungmann's observations bring to the fore two important points regarding the phrase *Mysterium Fidei*. The first is that it is in the earliest accounts, and therefore, it has longevity. Also, while St. Thomas' assertion that the *Mysterium Fidei* was given by Our Lord and comes to us via the Apostles cannot be verified without further texts or witness on the side of the Fathers, nevertheless, the obscurity of its origin places this element of the liturgy in the same category as those things which have been discussed prior in this text. When there is doubt, the favor is on the side of the tradition. We cannot fully dismiss what St. Thomas says, nor can we confirm it. But it is precisely that St. Thomas' explanation is plausible, which would mean that the pope as a matter of prudence would adopt the practice of when in doubt, favor goes to the tradition.

The second thing of interest regarding Jungmann's assertion is that it is not history that the *Mysterium Fidei* was pronounced by the deacon. In recent times, the *Mysterium Fidei* was moved outside the words of Consecration, perhaps from the motive of not being able to verify these statements of St. Thomas in the Fathers,[57] but also

---

[54]Ibid., p. 199f.

[55]See ibid., p. 200f.

[56]See ibid., p. 200, footnote, 33.

[57]In this author's research, the references of the Fathers to this was not able to be verified. This would imply that the theological note of this particular element of the liturgy being in the words of Consecration would not enjoy the same level of certitude as other particular elements. This being said, however, it

because of the adoption of the principle that favor does *not* go to the tradition, when in matters of doubt. The principle that was adopted is that modern man is different and by extension is more capable of judging what should and should not be in the liturgy than what was handed to them from the tradition. However, the fact that certain ecclesiastics did not follow the principle that when in matters of doubt, favor falls to the tradition, would not exempt the pope from following it as a matter of prudence.

D. Preface

One last particular which we will discuss here has to do with the Preface. Gihr observes:

> To trace the origin of the Preface and its introduction into the sacrificial rite, one must go back to the days of the apostles; this apostolic origin of the Preface is evident from the testimony of the Fathers, and especially from the most ancient liturgies, not a single one of which can be found without a Preface. The oriental liturgies have had from the beginning until the present time but a single Preface. In the West, on the contrary, the number of Prefaces, even at an early date, increased to such a degree, that before the time of St. Gregory the Great almost every formula of the Mass contained a separate Preface.[58]

According to Gihr, the fact that the Mass has a Preface goes back to the Apostles, *i.e.*, that the rite of Mass is to have a Preface enjoys the quality of Apostolicity. Here Gihr is resting it on two essential pieces

---

does have the quality of longevity, insofar as it has been in the liturgical texts from very early on, and a fruitful study would be to trace its lineage through the liturgical texts.

[58]Gihr, *Holy Sacrifice of the Mass*, p. 553.

of evidence. The first is that there is testimony among the patristics that the Preface is of Apostolic origin. The second is the fact that it is found in all of the most ancient liturgies. The assertion here rests on the principle that if something is contained in all of the texts from the most ancient of times, then it comes via the Apostles. If Gihr is correct, given that all ritual texts of the Mass for the earliest times had a Preface (longevity) and that Fathers testify that it came from the Apostles (Apostolicity), then it would not be within the authority of the pope to promulgate a liturgy that lacked a Preface. Not that this has ever been done, and ultimately, that is not the point. The point is that when it comes to specific or particular things in the liturgy, the pope is likewise under restrictions of his authority in various ways and to various degrees.

Conclusion

Only a few examples of particulars are given in this chapter. However, it would simply not be possible to go into all of the various elements of the liturgy to give them the same level analysis, given the scope of this book. However, what was important to note is that there are varying levels of support for particular elements, but that even when there is not a high level of support, favor must fall to the tradition. One cannot but help to conclude that even now the liturgical studies are not as advanced as is necessary or desirable. Going forward, much more study needs to be done, and it would be best not to make a number of changes until more can be ascertained about the various elements and even then, having the knowledge of the elements does not give one latitude to change them. In fact, the knowledge may restrict the individual in that regard. However, in all of these matters reverence for the prior forms should be shown.

Chapter VII: Observations by Some Moderns

Since the advent of the liturgical movement that began in the late 1800s, a proliferation of writing has been done on the liturgy. There has also been a fair amount of commentary by modern theologians about a proper disposition and attitude toward the liturgy. There is a general tenor among the popes and theologians of the time, to adhere to what was given and be slow to adopt liturgical changes. As will be seen, even popes were drawing attention to certain difficulties in relation to certain individuals' attitudes toward the liturgy.

At the foundation of a proper understanding of the liturgy is how it relates to doctrine, as we have seen in relation to how the faith determines the liturgy, but also that heretics strive to change the liturgy to conform it to their errors. This brings to the fore the reality of the intimate relation between the Church's doctrine and her religious practice. We have already seen observations from Oppenheim, yet he draws attention to the fact that the liturgy is a *regula fidei*[1] as well as a *locus theologicus*[2] as an expression of the Deposit of Faith.[3] This would not change our understanding that what we believe determines how we worship, but the liturgical texts throughout time do constitute a part of the monuments of tradition. In this regard, they tend to give us an understanding of the faith of those who went before us.

One aspect that is understood in the tradition, but not often discussed, is how the liturgy forms the minds of the faithful on many levels. The first way is what was just discussed, *viz.*, that the content of the liturgy intellectually forms people in what they are to believe as

---

[1]Oppenheim, *Institutiones Systematico-Historica in Sacram Liturgiam*, Vol. VII, Principia Theologiae Liturgiae, p. 73.

[2]Ibid., p. 66.

[3]Ibid., p. 65.

to the doctrines of the faith. The liturgy does serve a catechetical function in that regard. What the Magisterium places before the faithful on a regular basis in the liturgy will determine what the laity think is the truth about the doctrines of the faith. Second, what they stress in the liturgy also tells the faithful what takes priorities in our belief. If a liturgy stresses sacrifice as opposed to the communal meal aspect or vice versa, those elements of the liturgy will form the people in how they are to approach their own spiritual lives. In other words, are they to focus on a life of sacrifice or one of community? Not that these are mutually exclusive, but if one is stressed over the other, it will result in different approaches, even in the spiritual lives of the faithful. The third is precisely that: the liturgy forms the spiritual lives of the faithful in a specific way. Anyone familiar with the different rites sees that the various liturgies form the respective faithful in different ways in their spiritual lives. This is one of the reasons why it is difficult for priests to offer two different rites, because the spiritual approaches, while compatible, are different and it can lead to a bifurcation in the priest's spiritual life. Even when a priest makes a change in rites, there is a shift in the priest's interior life.[4] Hence, the pope in any liturgical change must take into consideration the profound impact it will have on the spiritual lives of the laity as well as the priests.

Fourth, the various elements of the liturgy form the laity in the various virtues,[5] but above all, in how the virtue of religion is to be practiced and developed. For example, how people are instructed to receive Holy Communion can have a direct impact on how they see God is to be handled. How the elements of mystery are manifested as

---

[4]This author, along with numerous other priests, have noticed this reality, when priests who begin offering the ancient form of the liturgy notice a deepening in their sacrificial and priestly identity.

[5]Regarding various virtues and how the different rites bring about a different formation, see Ripperger, *Topics on Tradition*, passim.

well as how sacred things are approached and handled have a direct bearing on *how* people will develop Fear of the Lord and in some cases even develop it at all. Even the liturgical changes themselves teach the laity something about the attitude of the Magisterium toward the liturgy.

> Hence the many changes and additions of the text of the Canon, which were produced during the Middle Ages, have disappeared partly already wholly since the reform of St. Pius V, in 1570. Since the thirteenth century, the Canon is, therefore, through its origin, antiquity and use, venerable and inviolable and sacred. If ever a prayer of the Church came into existence under the special inspiration of the Holy Ghost, it is assuredly the prayer of the Canon. It is pervaded throughout by the spirit of faith, and permeated with the sweet odor of devotion; it is a holy work, full of force and unction. Its simple language, by its pithiness and its antique and Scriptural stamp, produces a touching effect on the mind of him who prays and offers the Sacrifice; it charms the soul, just like the dimly lit ancient, venerable basilicas of the Eternal City. Is it not a pleasure and a joy to the heart, that we still utter the very same words at the altar which so many devout and holy priests throughout the entire Church and in all ages have always used in praying and offering the Sacrifice? Already in the times of the Martyrs and in the chapels of the Catacombs these prayers of the Canon of the Mass were recited and sanctified.[6]

In the past, the attitude toward the liturgical forms was such that one had great reverence and awe for them. Rather than an attitude of subjecting its forms to one's own desires, whims or the spirit of the age, one approached it with an attitude of not just Fear of Lord, but of Piety. It was a holy thing, a sacred thing. It was not something to

---

[6]Gihr, *Holy Sacrifice of the Mass*, p. 581.

lay one's hands on and start making changes, but one which was to be venerated. After all, it was the liturgy said by thousands of saints, popes, bishops and priests before us. As God saw it offered, He saw its full context each and every time: He saw every saint that ever said it, every act of devotion made in it, etc. Basic humility left one recognizing one's unworthiness to change it, save by the command of the pope alone and even then with a certain "fear and trepidation." The individual entrusted with proposing the changes to the Holy Father was literally making suggestions about a liturgy said millions of times to the pleasure of God and that was about to affect the manner in which literally billions of people pray. This is not something to be taken lightly, nor according to one's own preferences, dispositions or desires. Since it had been said by so many in the past and had undergone such a slow development at the pleasure of God Himself, it was viewed as inviolable, if for no other reason than that sheer humility would require one to approach it knowing full well one's own inadequacies, inabilities and imperfections which one could easily introduce into the liturgy without the perfect guidance of God Himself.

The attitude shared by some who wanted to change the liturgy was already warned against by Pope Gregory the XVI to the bishop of Fribourg.

> As we have the opportunity of writing you, we cannot refrain from indicating to you another point that requires particular vigilance on the part of your Fraternity: especially those very priests whom we have already mentioned above who, taken in by novelty, do not fear to undervalue sacred rights and criticize the venerable usages of the Church, nor spare any effort to induce you, Venerable Brother, to publish a new Ritual that will satisfy their desires. But, conscious of your duty, watch constantly over the institutions of the ancient and never allow your clergy to depart from any prescription of the Ritual of the Holy Roman Church or from any rule that may

> have been inserted in any other Ritual you use, provided that the Ritual be ancient and approved by the lawful authority. We trust, Venerable Brother, that you will take this advice to heart in all obedience; and knowing that there have been changes in this field, we exhort and beseech you in our Lord not to delay in suppressing and correcting the innovations introduced.[7]

This quote is important if for no other reason than to show that the desire to change the liturgy to suit novelty has been a perennial problem and that what has been seen in the last 70 years was not something that was isolated or which occurred without any antecedent cause.

Pope Pius XII also re-iterated this same observation by Pope Gregory XVI:

> Indeed, though we are sorely grieved to note, on the one hand, that there are places where the spirit, understanding or practice of the sacred liturgy is defective, or all but inexistent, we observe with considerable anxiety and some misgiving, that elsewhere certain enthusiasts, over-eager in their search for novelty, are straying beyond the path of sound doctrine and prudence.[8]

From what Pope Pius XII has said, we can see that a liturgy, and by extension any liturgical change, must conform to sound doctrine and prudence. But he too warns against novelty, and this has been a

---

[7]Gregory XVI, (as found in *The Liturgy,* p. 119) Letter *Dolorem, quo jam diu*, November 30, 1839, to the Bishop of Fribourg.

[8]Pius XII, *Mediator Dei*, para. 8: "Iamvero, si ex una parte valde dolemus nonnullis in regionibus sacrae Liturgiae sensum, intellegentiam ac studium mancum interdum esse ac fere nullum, ex altera vero multa cum sollicitudine, non timoris vacua, animadvertimus nonnullos novitatis nimio studiosiores esse, atque ex rectae doctrinae ac prudentiae via transversos aberrare."

common theme that the Church has dealt with historically. It was already shown above that heretics strive to change the liturgy, but they often do so by incorporating novelty into the liturgy.

Novelty is that which is opposed to tradition, since novelty by nature supplants or contradicts the tradition.[9] Novelty is considered bad in the history of the Church, because it breaks the continuity of tradition. Our salvation depends upon tradition, since continuity in tradition is that by which the means of salvation are passed on from generation to generation and to as many people as possible. Moreover, the continuity of tradition ensures that each generation will inherit the wealth of patrimony of the saints.

One of the best writers on the topic of novelty is St. Vincent of Lerins in his work the *Commonitorium* written in 437 A.D. St. Vincent provides the following principle to begin the discussion of novelty in a text we saw before:

> In the Catholic Church itself, great care must be taken, that we hold that which has been believed everywhere, always, and by all. For this is truly and properly Catholic, which, as the force and notion of the name declares, almost all universally comprehend. But this at last becomes consent, if we follow the universal antiquity. Moreover, we follow universality in this way: if we confess that one true faith, which the whole Church throughout the world confesses; such is it with antiquity, if from those senses we in no way depart from what is manifest by our holy ancestors and fathers celebrated; so also it is the same with consent, if we adhere to the definitions and beliefs of all or almost all priests and doctors in that same antiquity.[10]

---

[9]This section is taken from *Ripperger, Topics on Tradition*, p. 25-31.

[10]St. Vincent of Lerins, *Commonitorium*, para. II: "in ipsa item Catholica Ecclesia magnopere curandum est ut id teneamus quod ubique, quod semper, quod ab omnibus creditum est. Hoc est etenim vere proprieque catholicum, quod ipsa

St. Vincent essentially establishes that the principle of judgment about what we are to believe is that which we have received from "our holy ancestors and fathers." In effect, it is tradition, *i.e.*, that which has been handed on to us, which constitutes what we are to believe. For there is no aspect of what we believe as Catholics that was not passed on to us from those who went before us.

> For that holy and prudent man knew that to admit the notion of piety is nothing other than that everything is received by faith from the fathers and consigned by the same faith to the sons and [piety is] not our religion, which we want, that leads but more that which leads must be followed, for it is proper to Christian modesty and gravity not to pass on his own beliefs to those who come after him, but to preserve what has been received from his ancestors. What then was the issue of the whole matter? What but the usual and customary one? Antiquity was retained, novelty was rejected.[11]

Tradition requires that we accept what is given to us and pass it on

---

vis nominis ratioque declarat, quae omnia fere universiter comprehendit. Sed hoc ita demum fiet, si sequamur universitatem antiquitatem, consensionem. Sequemur autem universitatem hoc modo, si hanc unam fidem veram esse fateamur quam tota per orbem terrarum confitetur ecclesia; antiquitatem vero ita, si ab his sensibus nullatenus recedamus quos sanctos majores ac patres nostros celebrasse manifestum est: consensionem quoque itidem, si, in ipsa vetustate, omnium vel certe pene omnium sacerdotum pariter et magistrorum definitiones sententiasque sectemur."

[11]St. Vincent of Lerins, *Commonitorium*, para. VI: "Intelligebat etenim vir sanctus et prudens, nihil aliud rationem pietatis admittere, nisi ut omnia, qua fide a patribus suscepta forent, eadem fide filiis consignarentur, nosque religionem non, qua vellemus, ducere, set potius, qua illa duceret, sequi oportere, idque esse proprium christianae modestiae et gravitatis, non sua posteris tradere sed a maioribus accepta servare. Quis ergo tunc universi negotii exitus? Quis utique, nisi usitatus et solitus? Retenta est scilicet antiquitas, explosa novitas."

intact without passing on our own teaching. Catholic tradition does not admit of a Hegelian view that things must always change and cannot help but change. Rather, the Catholic tradition holds that those things necessary for salvation will not change, even until the end of time.

When novelty arises, confusion ensues. As St. Vincent says:

> Not only from the example of Photinus but also Apollinaris do we learn the danger of ecclesiastical temptation and at the same time we warn by observing to diligently keep custody of the faith. For he gave rise to great burning and great agitation among his disciples; the Church's authority drawing them one way, their master's influence the opposite; so that, wavering and tossed hither and thither between the two, they did not know what to choose.[12]

One of the effects of novelty, *i.e.*, heresy, is that it tends not to clarify what the Church has always believed, but to confuse the faithful. "In the Church of God the teacher's error is the people's trial, a trial by so much the greater in proportion to the greater learning of the erring teacher."[13] This applies not only to priests or confessors but also to members of the Magisterium. If a member or some members of the Magisterium deny or contradict a traditional teaching of the Church, great confusion will affect the faithful until the teaching is reaffirmed with clarity. We may say that if a pope were to do so, as in the case of Pope John XXII regarding the particular judgment, it would cause

---

[12]Ibid., para. XI: "Neque solum Photini sed etiam Apollinaris exemplo istius Ecclesiasticae tentationis periculum discimus, et simul ad observandae diligentius fidei custodiam commonemur. Etenim ipse auditoribus suis magnos aestus et magnas generavit augustias; quippe com eos huc Ecclesiae traheret auctoritas, huc magistri retraheret consuetudo; eumque inter utraque nutabundi et fluctuantes, quid potius sibi seligendum foret non expedirent."

[13]Ibid.

the greatest of confusions, since it is the office of the papacy above all that is to guarantee the clarity of what is taught in the Church and the continuity of the tradition.

What then are the principles by which one can detect whether something is a novelty? St. Vincent observes that when something is passed on, beginning with the ancestors and coming to our own day, "this rather should be the result, there should be no discrepancy between the first and the last."[14] The core teachings of the tradition should remain the same from the time of the death of the last Apostle until now. Therefore, if there is any contradiction between what the tradition has *always* held and the new teaching, the teaching is a novelty and is to be rejected.

This applies whether it is a matter of principle or of conclusion. When it is a matter of principle, the new teaching will contradict some formally defined teaching or some part of the Creed, *e.g.*, if one were to say that Christ became reincarnated and did not resurrect, that would be contrary to the line of the Creed which states that "He rose from the dead." Therefore, Christological reincarnation would be a novelty. When it is a matter of conclusion, a conclusion from the novelty would contradict some traditional teaching of the Church. For example, if someone were to say that Christ did not know He was God, the conclusion would be that He did not know that He was the Savior since only God can save.

Another way of determining whether a teaching is a novelty is when it is a teaching that has never heretofore been taught, *i.e.*, it is a completely new doctrine. Here we are not talking about valid conclusions drawn from traditional teachings, but one which has no real connection as such to the teachings. For example, if one were to assert that there is an eighth sacrament, one would know that this teaching is a novelty. Authentic development of doctrine always provides a clearer understanding of the constant teachings of the

---

[14]Ibid., c. 23: "consequens est ut primis atque extremis sibimet non discrepantibus."

Church. Novelty does not, as we saw in the quote above from St. Vincent. Therefore, one of the ways of knowing that a teaching is a novelty is if it leads to greater confusion among the faithful. While this is not a hard and fast rule, since sometimes abstract but valid conclusions in theology can leave some faithful who are not very knowledgeable or intelligent confused, nevertheless, a novelty never begets clarity of intellectual vision regarding the teachings of the Church.

Another way to know whether something is a novelty is to see the effect it has on the spiritual lives of those who follow the novelty. If the new teaching makes people holier, more than likely it is an authentic development, *e.g.*, St. John of the Cross' doctrine on detachment is a greater clarification of the teachings known since the time of Christ or even before. Those who follow St. John's teaching become holier. But a novel teaching will tend to adversely affect one's spiritual life. For example, if one were to propose that the Precious Blood should be poured down the sacrarium or back into a jug containing wine, rather than reverently consumed, this would be a sacrilegious practice, a novelty, and harmful to people's faith in the Real Presence and harmful to them spiritually. So if the teaching is a clarification, it will help people to lead more Catholic lives than before, whereas if it is a novelty, it will erode people's spiritual lives.

St. Vincent provides another principle to determine whether something is a novel teaching and that is when the terminology changes, *i.e.,* the people use new words.[15] Great care must be taken regarding this principle, however, for there have been times in history when new words were introduced which actually clarified the teaching, *e.g.,* the word *transubstantiation* was a term "coined by the theologians of the 12th century (Magister Roland [who later became Pope Alexander III] about 1150, Stephen of Tournai about 1160,

---

[15]See ibid., c. 24.

Petrus Comestor 1160-1170)."[16] This term greatly clarified the reality of the change of substance in the Eucharist. But, at other times, authors will introduce new terms which actually reflect a heretical mind. For example, the term "transignification" was a theological term introduced which denied that there is a substantial change in the Eucharist but merely a change in meaning to those attending Mass. We must also be on guard against those who change the meaning of traditional terms to something which is heretical. For example, some have changed the meaning of the term "revelation." Traditionally, public revelation ended with the death of the last Apostle. Today, some theologians use the term "revelation" to mean an ongoing manifestation of God to man or an ongoing process by which man comes to a better understanding of himself, which is contrary to the continuity of the tradition and the very nature of revelation.

St. Paul in his first epistle to Timothy (6:20) says, "O Timothy, guard the Deposit, avoiding profane novelties of words and oppositions of science falsely so called."[17] Those introducing novelties will often use pseudo-science in order to undermine the traditional teaching so that there is no opposition to the introduction of the novel teaching. They will use a false science or a false conclusion from a science in order to contradict some teaching of the tradition. For example, the use of Darwinian evolutionary theory is often used as a means of undermining the traditional teaching of all men descending from Adam and Eve and the doctrine of original sin. The novel teaching is called polygenesis and it was condemned by Pius XII.[18] The scientific foundations for Darwinian evolution are clearly in question and there is question as to whether it is truly scientific as a

---

[16]Ludwig Ott, *Fundamentals of Catholic Dogma*, p. 379.

[17]Translation is by the author from the Vulgate: "O Timothee depositum custodi devitans profanas vocum novitates et oppositiones falsi nominis scientiae."

[18]Pius XII, *Humanae Generis*, para. 37.

theory.[19]

These are some of the means by which one can know whether a teaching is a novelty or not. Even though we must be on guard against novelty, we must also accept the clearly traditional understanding that over the course of time, members of the Church have given greater precision to the expression of certain doctrines through theological endeavors. Moreover, the rejection of novelties does not of itself reject the possibility that the changes mentioned are not possible. What rejection of novelties does mean, however, is that (a) the members of the Church, particularly the Magisterium, must be on guard against heresy/novelty, and (b) changes must follow authentic Catholic principles.

Development of teaching is possible only when it is homogenous, *i.e.*, what is believed by our Fathers is the same as what we believe today. While we might have a more precise expression of some doctrine, such as in the teaching of the term "transubstantiation," what the Fathers and Doctors of the Church believed before is identical to what we ought to believe today. Homogenous development also means that any conclusions which a theologian may draw from the Deposit of Faith must follow logical rules. The conclusions cannot assert what is denied in the premises. For example, one cannot assert that since God is all merciful (premise), He could never damn anyone to the eternal punishment of hell (conclusion), since one of the principles or teachings of the Church is that God is also infinitely just (premise), which requires that should someone die in the state of mortal sin, he should be condemned for his sin (conclusion). Greater precision in the method of theology helps one to see with greater clarity the same truth as the truth held by our ancestors. Just as better glasses help one to see what one saw before with greater clarity, so greater precision over time has helped the members of the Church to see the truth of what has been revealed.

---

[19]There is a whole host of literature available on this question, but for an example, see Behe, *Darwin's Black Box*.

If the pair of glasses one wears blurs what one sees or changes what one sees (such as in the case of rose colored glasses), one should take off those glasses and don a pair that will help him to see better. In like manner, when one finds himself in a period of novelty, the novelty can obscure his intellectual vision, and so he must return to the constant teaching of the Church, *i.e.,* to tradition in order to have a greater grasp of the truths of the faith. Theological development should not cause one to reject the faith, but move one to a more firm assent to the truths that are revealed.

True intellectual advance is only possible by the handing on of tradition, not only in theology, but in all fields of science. If the prior generation had never passed on to the current generation any of the knowledge they had of the empirical sciences, we would not enjoy the knowledge in the empirical sciences that we do today. In like manner, in theology, we must stand on the shoulders of our predecessors and use the advances that they made so that we can continue the advance. If we do not do so, we run the risk of intellectual stagnation and ignorance. The virtue of faith will help us to see the greatness of our forefathers and the theological work that they did, such as St. Thomas, St. Augustine, and all of the Doctors of the Church. When tradition is rejected, one rejects the work that was already accomplished, the homogenous development is rejected and our understanding of the faith is lessened. Therefore, the science of theology can only advance when theologians stand on the theological work and accomplishments of the saints and build upon that work.

This is why we must look at the Deposit of Faith through the eyes of the past. While it is possible for theological precision to increase our understanding of some aspect of faith and the Church has defined doctrines, which give greater clarity and which settle disputes, that judgment is still done by looking back to the tradition for the foundation of those judgments. The eyes and direction of one's sight remain the same, the glasses improve our vision.

In the context of the liturgy, it means that novelty in the doctrinal sense will not have any place in the liturgy. In the context of liturgical development itself, novelty would also have no place in the liturgy. Two conclusions can be drawn from this. The first is that the liturgy should only organically develop where the substance remains the same. If a liturgy is introduced which has no organic connection to the ritual that went before it, it will leave the faithful with the impression that the theology of the Church has changed. Second, the pope would have the obligation from the Divine Positive Law (from the precept to confirm the brethren) not to introduce a rite that was not organically developed from a prior rite that has the quality of Apostolicity. The pope would also be bound by the obligations of prudence which would avoid substantial changes to the ritual in order to avoid confusion in the laity. Also, by preserving those elements that enjoy longevity, he will be more assured of the Will of God being served in any liturgical change.

If a rite of the Mass were to be introduced that had substantial changes and did not slowly and organically develop in the *accidentalia*, the pope would run the risk of placing the laity in a psychological position which would favor heresy. This is one of the basic gists of this entire discussion on novelty. Even if a new liturgy did not contain anything contrary to the faith, it can leave people with the impression that the faith is changing, and this will slowly lead people toward falling into error in their thinking.

Novelty also runs the danger of locking the Church into a "time warp," so to speak. A time warp is "a hypothetical discontinuity or distortion occurring in the flow of time that would move events from one time period to another or suspend the passage of time." In other words, because novelty comes from the people of a certain era, it often locks people into the mindset and thinking of that era. If the novelty is maintained, the Church does not move on with the passage of time, ironically not keeping up with the times; but it also loses the perennial character in the liturgy, which has the ability to appeal to all generations of all time. In effect, it is only when the Church maintains the Apostolicity, longevity, and perennial characteristics of the liturgy, only making minor changes to the *accidentalia* of the liturgy, that it actually does "keep up with the times" and appeal to every generation. Even if one adheres to the idea that the Church should adapt to the times, the problem is the perception of the time to which one adapts and the danger of locking the Church into a time warp. While the teaching of each generation requires a process by which the Deposit of Faith is adequately explained, the Deposit itself does not change and certain formulations do not change. What changes is not the Church adapting to the times, but striving to make the Gospel known to each generation, so that the generation can adapt to the Church's perennial teaching and worship. In effect, the Church must strive to adapt the times to the Church, not the Church to the times. Adapting the Church and liturgy to the times will lock it into a time warp; whereas, helping each generation adapt to the Church's perennial teachings and worship will help each generation to be lifted out of the limitations of the times. From all of this, we are reminded of the quote from Pope Benedict the XVI, "What earlier generations held as sacred, remains sacred and great for us too, and it cannot be all of a sudden entirely forbidden or even considered harmful."[20]

---

[20] *Summorum Pontificum.*

Chapter VIII: Papal Suppression of a Rite

The recent events in relation to the ancient rite of Mass in the context of *Traditiones Custodes* and what is referred to as the clarification has some faithful wondering if the pope intends to eventually suppress the rite. The question about whether he would have the authority to suppress the ancient rite of Mass, sometimes referred to as the rite of St. Gregory the Great as well as other names, will not be addressed here. What will be addressed is if the pope has the right to suppress a rite, and if so under what conditions. For that reason, we must revisit certain texts and concepts discussed throughout this book in a different light.

I. The Authority of the Pope to Suppress a Rite

In a prior quote of the Council of Trent, we read:

> It declares furthermore, that in the dispensation of the sacraments, "salva illorum substantia," the Church may, according to circumstances, times and places, determine or change whatever she may judge most expedient for the benefit of those receiving them or for the veneration of the sacraments; and this power has always been hers.[1]

This passage essentially shows that the Church has authority to change the liturgy "except those which pertain to the substance" of the sacraments. If the Church has authority to "determine" (to use the word of the Council of Trent) the liturgy, she would have the authority to suppress a rite for the benefit of the faithful. Since the

---

[1]Council of Trent, Session 22, c. 7 (Denz. 931): "Praeterea declarat hanc potestatem perpetuo in ecclesia fuisse ut in sacramentorum dispensatione salva illorum substantia ea statueret vel mutaret quae suscipientium utilitati seu ipsorum sacramentorum venerationi pro rerum temporum et locorum varietate magis expedire iudicaret."

plenitude of authority in relation to matters of discipline,[2] (which flows from his supreme jurisdiction,[3]) of which the liturgy are a part, belongs to the office of the papacy, then the pope would have the authority to suppress a rite. We have already noted that the pope would even have the obligation to suppress a rite, if it violated the Natural Law and we may also say the Divine Positive Law.

We also saw in a prior quote of Pope Pius XII, his statement that:

> the Sovereign Pontiff alone enjoys the right to recognize and establish any practice touching the worship of God, to introduce and approve new rites, as also to modify those he judges to require modification.[4]

Again, the pope has the plenitude of power in matters of discipline, which follows from his supreme jurisdiction. It is based upon the documents of the Church and the popes, as well as the general consensus of Theologians that the pope does have the authority to suppress a rite.

II. Particular Instances

In the history of the Church, there have been a few instances where the pope did suppress certain rites. Oppenheim recounts the

---

[2]Denz. 1827. See also Ott, *Fundamentals of Catholic Dogma*, p. 285: "The Pope possesses full and supreme power of jurisdiction over the whole Church, not merely in matters of faith and morals, but also in Church discipline and in the government of the Church. (*De Fide*.)"

[3]Denz. 1831.

[4]Pius, XII, *Mediator Dei*, para. 58: "Quamobrem uni Summo Pontifici ius est quemlibet de divino cultu agendo morem recognoscere ac statuere, novos inducere ac probare ritus, eosque etiam immutare, quos quidem immutandos iudicaverit."

fact that Gregory VII suppressed the Mozarabic liturgy in Spain which contained errors.[5] It is a well known fact that Pope St. Pius V suppressed numerous rites which were less than 200 years old. The real question is: Are there conditions to which the pope is bound when suppressing a rite?

III. Principles Governing Papal Suppression of a Rite

A. Against the Divine Positive Law and Natural Law

It has already been noted that the pope would have the obligation to suppress a rite, if the rite violated the Divine Positive Law or Natural Law. We just noted that the pope would have the right to suppress a rite, if the example of St. Gregory is an indicator, if the rite contained (theological) error. Conversely, he would not be permitted to suppress a rite, if in doing so, in some manner, it violated the Divine Positive Law or Natural Law.

B. The Rite Lacks Apostolicity

When we look at the history of Pope St. Pius V's suppression of the various rites, a few things come to surface as to the reasons why, and these reasons provide a foundation for the principles governing the pope in the suppression of a rite. In chapter four, we saw that certain elements of the liturgy come from the Apostles themselves or are reported by the Fathers as coming from the Apostles. These elements would be required to be in a rite of the Mass, as was discussed. When Pope Pius V suppressed the rites, one of the principles for suppressing them was their lack of Apostolicity. In fact, his codification of the Mass, which has been used for 460 years, was based upon the fact that the rite could demonstrate its Apostolic quality.

---

[5]Oppenheim, *Principia Theologiae Liturgiae*, p. 52: "*S. Gregorius VII* (1073-1085) in Hispania Liturgiam mozarabicam suppressit, qui Adoptanorum errores videbatur continere."

> In its essential elements it dates back to St. Gregory the Great, from which it is also called the Gregorian rite, a more correct but not exhaustive name, because the rite dates back even before Gregory the Great to apostolic times. ...From the account of the Acts of the Apostles we can deduce the existence of a simple but fixed ritual that was essentially complete and that was followed uniformly by the apostles and their collaborators. ...These apostolic prescriptions had the authority of law, since in the first half of the second century the apologist St. Justin attests to the fidelity with which it was followed in the description he gave of the Mass of his time.[6]

What separated the rite as coming from St. Gregory the Great in his codification via Pope Pius V was the reality that the rite could trace its lineage or was shown to contain those elements that were known to be of Apostolic origin. Pope Pius V, then was able to suppress the rites, which contained elements that could not demonstrate this lineage or quality. In fact,

> it is even more precious because of the fact that it attests to the ritual practice of the Roman Church, in which, as St. Irenaeus († 202) writes "the tradition that has come from the apostles is faithfully guarded." ...The documentation of the individual parts of our Canon dates back to at least the fifth century, and obliges us to identify it in its broad outlines with what the ancients held to be of apostolic tradition.[7]

It is for this reason that De Mattei observes that:

---

[6]De Mattei, *Saint Pius V*, p. 308.

[7]Ibid., p. 309. Ibid., p. 310f: "The Mass in the High Middle Ages was already considered an inviolable inheritance. Even more, it was commonly held that it dated back to the apostles and that it was written by St. Peter Himself."

> All of the doctrine on the Mass of the Council of Trent is contained in the bull *Quo Primum* of Pius V, which did not introduce anything new but restored the worship of the Church to its integrity, after being disfigured by Protestants and humanists in the preceding fifty years.[8]

As will be seen in the section on longevity below, the real issue was that those rites which had proliferated within 200 years prior contained elements that could not be demonstrated in the tradition, nor were they of Apostolic lineage. Hence, Pope Pius V considered it within his authority or right to suppress those rites.

There is, therefore, a twofold understanding to take away from Pope Pius V's suppression of certain rites. The first is that, if a rite contains elements that lack Apostolicity, he may suppress the rite, provided the other considerations below obtain. In other words, if there are elements that came from the Apostles according to the Fathers or by Revelation, then if a rite lacks those elements, the pope may suppress that rite. He could reform the rite and insert those elements, if certain other conditions such as prudence are in place, but he would have the authority to suppress it. The second form is that if a rite has those elements that can be clearly demonstrated to have come from the Apostles, either by patristic testimony or by Revelation, the pope can only suppress it if other conditions are in place. In other words, if those elements are in a rite, he must first make other determinations before one could say he is within his authority to suppress that rite.

C. Contrary to Prudence

In chapter five, prudence was discussed and how the pope would be bound by the Natural Law in relation to prudence and by the Divine Positive Law in relation to supernatural prudence. When we look at the instances in which popes suppressed rites in the past, aside

---

[8]Ibid., p. 311.

from the foregoing, we also see another aspect that comes into consideration.

> The Roman Missal desired by the Council of Trent was promulgated by Pius V with the bull *Quo Primum* of July 19, 1570. The expressions "Tridentine Mass" or "Mass of St. Pius V" by which the rite codified by Pius V is known are improper, because the pope did nothing else than wisely fix and set limitations on a rite that had already been in use in Rome for centuries.[9]

Aside from the principles mentioned above when Pope St. Pius V promulgated *Quo Primum* and suppressed the rites, which did enjoy Apostolicity in its elements, there was an element of prudence also involved. When rites have a certain longevity, they tend to have a spiritual impact on the members of the Church in such a manner that changing them can result in disturbances among the faithful as was discussed prior in the text. What this essentially boils down to is that the pope ought not suppress a rite willy nilly or without grave cause, as this would be against the Divine Positive Law to confirm the brethren. It would also be contrary to prudence.

D. Contrary to Tradition

The discussion of the tradition as normative in the considerations of making changes also comes to bear on the question of suppressing a rite.

> But it is even more precious because of the fact that it attests to the ritual practice of the Roman Church, in which, as St. Irenaeus († 202) writes "the tradition that has come from the

---

[9]De Mattei, *Saint Pius V*, p. 308. Cf. *Missale Romanum* in the fore document *Cum Sanctissimum eucharistiae Sacramentorum,* (Clemens Papa VIII ad perpetuam rei memoriam) of M. Vessyrius Barnianus (July 7, 1604.)

> apostles is faithfully guarded."[10] ...There is moreover a constant tradition that St. Gregory was last to touch the essential part of the Mass, namely the Canon. Benedict (1740-1758) says: "No Pope has added to or changed the Canon since St. Gregory." Even if the rite of the Mass continued to develop in its nonessential parts after the era of St. Gregory, Fr. Fortescue explains that "all later modifications were fitted into the old arrangement and the most important parts were not touched. From, roughly, the time of St. Gregory we have the text of the Mass, its order and arrangement, as a sacred tradition that no one ventured to touch except in unimportant details."[11]

While this quote is dealing with the changes made to the Mass, the principle embodied in the quote is also that the rite itself is to be faithfully guarded. In other words, it is not just the case that the rite not be changed except in the *accidentalia*, but that Pope Pius V took what went before him, restored the rite of the Mass based upon the original or ancient texts, and therefore, did not see himself as starting a completely new rite, but as restoring and re-codifying the use of what was part of the tradition. When considering the suppression of the Mass, the pope would not see himself as suppressing something, which was part of the tradition, but rather those things which were not. He suppressed various rites precisely because they did not bear

---

[10]Ibid., p. 309.

[11]Ibid., p. 310: (quoting Fortescue, *The Mass*, p. 173). Ibid., p. 312: "Pius V states that he has entrusted this difficult task to 'men of chosen doctrine. And these, indeed, after having diligently collected all of the codices recommended for their chastity and integrity – the old ones from Our Vatican Library and others sought out from every place – and having further consulted the writings of ancient and proven authors who have left us testimonies about the sacred ordering of the same rites, they have finally restored the Missal in its ancient form according to the norm and rite of the holy Fathers.'"

the stamp of tradition in the sense of longevity, but saw himself bound to restore the rite, based upon the tradition.[12] Given this, then *a fortiori*, he would not see himself as having the authority to suppress a rite, which could demonstrate itself to have originated in and to have developed organically within the tradition.

E. Contrary to Longevity

Hence, longevity played a key role in the judication of Pope St. Pius V, when considering which rites would remain and which would not.

> Pius V made this missal obligatory in all of the churches that could not prove an antiquity of two hundred years for their particular usage, as he had already done for the breviary.[13] ...The reform of Pius V consisted in "restoring the Roman Mass to its original purity, purging it of all its profane elements and things from the Renaissance that have invaded it in recent centuries."[14]

While it may appear that Pope St. Pius V set the cut off date of 200 years to preserve the Dominican rite, since that is his personal patrimony, this would not detract from the fact that his suppression of the other rites did proceed from sound principle.

Herein lies the point, namely, when the pope suppresses a rite, his authority is bound by the same principles, *mutatis mutandis*, as binding his authority and regulates it in relation to the changing of rites. He does not have the authority to suppress a rite willy nilly, as

---

[12]Ibid., p. 315: "The essence of the reform of St. Pius V was, like that of St. Gregory the Great, respect for tradition."

[13]Ibid., p. 313.

[14]Ibid., p. 314.

they say. Yet, the opposite is also true from the foregoing, *i.e.*, the pope would have the authority to suppress a rite which did not have the elements commanded by Our Lord, which come through the Apostles, or did not have the quality of Apostolicity in its elements, or lacked longevity as manifest in the tradition. Yet, if the pope were to suppress a rite, he would have the grave obligation to provide a rite, which did meet these requirements for those whose rite is suppressed. In other words, a pope could not suppress a rite and then not provide a rite for those priests and bishops who offered that rite, which met the above requirements. Historically, in the cases of St. Gregory the Great and St. Pius V^th^, this was done by the codification of a rite already in existence, *i.e.*, a prior rite, which could demonstrate its lineage back to the Apostles.[15] He would also not have the authority to suppress a rite, which did meet those requirements, in order to provide for them a new rite, which did not have those elements or which could not demonstrate its lineage back to the Apostles.

IV. Papal Imposition of a Rite

Can the pope impose a rite or promulgate a new rite? Here we repeat the quote of Pope Pius XII:

> the Sovereign Pontiff alone enjoys the right to recognize and establish any practice touching the worship of God, to introduce and approve new rites, as also to modify those he

---

[15]In a prior chapter it was observed that the true force behind the document *Quo Primum* of Pope St. Pius V, issued in 1570 was that a priest had a right to offer the rite of Mass that contained divine and divino-apostolic elements. Yet, if one observes the two historical instances in which rites were suppressed and imposed, the popes simply codified the rite which could trace its lineage back to the Apostles, which would support the idea that the priest would have a right to offer the the rite which was codified by Pope Gregory the Great and re-codified by Pope Pius V^th^, due to its Apostolicity and longevity as well.

> judges to require modification.[16]

What exactly is understood in prior documents in relation to "new rites," which the pope may introduce or approve? If the history and tradition are any indicator, the promulgation of new rites would encompass two forms. The first is as Pope St. Pius V did, in which he restored the traditional elements and removed elements which did not enjoy Apostolicity, longevity or tradition. This was considered a new Missal in the sense that it codified what went before and it removed things which were in various rites, which were no longer to continue in the rite of Mass. The second is when the pope would approve a new rite, as was seen in approving the rites of the various religious orders, which had variances from the Roman rite, but which contained the various required elements, such as the Dominican Rite, the Seraphic rite, the Carmelite Rite of the Holy Sepulcher, etc. The canon was virtually the same, but the Offertories were often different, while still containing the elements which come from the tradition. They would also include various saints in the calendars, which were not in the Roman Missal, since the Roman Missal was intended for use in the universal Church, despite it being proper to Rome. Whereas the rites proper to certain religious orders would often have the saints of the universal calendar of the Roman Missal, but also those saints proper to the religious order, which were not in the general calendar. These would be examples of new rites the pope would approve and promulgate.

If a pope were to promulgate a new rite, as appears to be the case in relation to the Missal of Pius V, could he impose it on the rest of the Church or on a certain segment of the Church? *Quo Primum* itself testifies to this authority of the pope to do so. Yet, he would still

---

[16]Pius, XII, *Mediator Dei*, para. 58: "Quamobrem uni Summo Pontifici ius est quemlibet de divino cultu agendo morem recognoscere ac statuere, novos inducere ac probare ritus, eosque etiam immutare, quos quidem immutandos iudicaverit."

be bound in his authority to only impose a rite of Mass that fulfills those requirements already discussed, *i.e.*, a codification of what went before.

Conclusion

Given the history of when popes have suppressed the rites of the Mass, this would not be something that is done in the normal course of things. It would be something extraordinarily rare and with good reason. The reasons given for suppressing prior rites had to do with the rites themselves, *i.e.*, there was something in them which was contrary to faith (the Divine Positive Law or Natural Law), divino-Apostolic tradition, etc. The suppressing of a rite was not done due to disagreements of the pope with a particular segment of the Church over matters that did not pertain to the faith, nor over the character of the people who attend the rite. In other words, a pope would not have the authority to suppress a rite because he does not happen to like a particular segment of the faithful or because he found them onerous. His authority would pertain to suppressing the rite because something in the rite itself lacks an essential requirement or one in which the *accidentalia* contain things contrary to the tradition. The fact that certain heretical rites were suppressed is based upon the heresy in the rite itself, independent of the heretics themselves. One suppresses rites, because of what is in the rites; one excommunicates or canonically sanctions heretics. These two are very different, and prudence itself requires proceeding differently in each case.

Chapter IX
Papal Reverence

Throughout the history of the Church, various documents have addressed the disposition that the Holy Father should have toward the ancient rites, which began with Christ and the Apostles and have been passed on throughout the history of the Church. Despite liturgical offshoots and times when various liturgical innovations were introduced, but then subsequently pruned, the core of that liturgical tradition remained. We quote, once again burdening the patience of the reader, the following observations made in prior chapters regarding the pope's obligation to "hold fast to the traditions,"[17] even regarding liturgical matters.

I. Various Authorities

In the context of the pope rejecting anything that pertains to Apostolicity, which was seen above, we read:

> If the pope is able to separate himself without some reasonable cause, but purely by his own will, from the body of the Church and the college of priests through the non-observance of those things which the universal Church observes from the tradition of the Apostles (according to the c. Ecclesi[astic]arum, dist. 11), or because of non-observance of those things which are universally ordained by the ecumenical councils or the authority of the Apostolic See, most of all which are ordained for divine worship, such as, by refusing to observe in himself those things which concern the universal state of the Church, or the universal rite of ecclesiastical worship, as if he were to refuse to celebrate in sacred vestments, or in consecrated places, or with candles, or to sign himself with the sign of the cross as does the rest of the college of priests, and similar

[17] 2 Thes. 2:15.

things, which seem generally ordered to perpetual advantage.[18]

We also observed that, if the pope were unfaithful in observing the liturgical rites, which came from the Apostles, some authors considered this to be of such import that it would separate him from the body of the Church. Suarez observes:

> ...The Pope could be schismatic, if he did not want to maintain the union and conjunction he should with the whole body of the Church, as if he tried to excommunicate the whole Church, or if he willed to overthrow all ecclesiastical ceremonies established by Apostolic tradition, which Cajetanus noted, 2.2, q. 39.[19]

These above quotes reflect a theological position which holds to the pope being bound, not just by the prior theological tradition, but even the liturgical tradition. The idea of a pope writing a completely new

---

[18]*Summa de ecclesia*, lib. IV, pars Ia, cap. xi, § Secundo sic (fol. 196v of the 1489 Roman edition, p. 552 of the 1560 Salamanca edition, and p. 369v of the 1561 Venice edition): "Si papa potest separare se sine aliqua rationabili causa, sed pura voluntate sua a corpore ecclesiae & collegio sacerdotum per non observantiam eorum quae universalis ecclesia ex traditione apostolorum observat: iuxta c. ecclesiarum. dist. 11, aut propter non observantiam eorum quae per universalia concilia, aut apostolicae sedis authoritatem sunt universaliter ordinata, maxime ad cultum divinum, ut puta nolendo observare in se ea quae universalem statum ecclesiae, aut universalem ritum cultus ecclesiastici concernunt, ut quod nollet celebrare in vestibus sacris, aut locis sacratis, aut cum luminaribus, aut signare se signo Crucis sicut residuum sacerdotum collegium facit, & similia, quae ad perpetuam generaliter ordinata videntur utilitatem."

[19]Suarez, *De Caritate*, XII, 1: "Et hoc secundo modo posset Papa esse schismaticus, si nollet tenere cum toto Ecclesiae corpore unionem et conjunctionem quam debet, ut si tentaret totam Ecclesiam excommunicare, aut si vellet omnes ecclesiasticas caeremonias apostolica traditione firmatas evertere, quod notavit Cajetanus, 2.2, q. 39."

rite that had no organic connection to the liturgical tradition, and lacked Apostolicity and longevity, would have been considered outside the scope of papal authority. Obviously, given the right conditions in the Church, the pope could do such a thing and impose it upon the faithful by the sheer psychological power of the papal office, but such action would not translate into him actually having the authority to do so.

The papal oath, thought to be used between the 7th and the 11th centuries, attests to the fact that keeping the liturgical rites as received was part of the pope's duties pertaining to his office:

> To keep the discipline and rite of the Church, as I have found it, and as I discovered it given by my Holy predecessors, inviolable. ...To keep the discipline and the rite, as we find it canonically handed down by my holy predecessors, as long as life is in them.[20]

It is precisely this papal oath as well as the subsequent disposition of the popes toward the liturgical tradition that resulted in the idea that the pope was bound to not make substantive changes to the ritual of the Mass and sacraments.[21] This is why even a "minor change," such

---

[20] *Patrologia Latina*, 105, 42C (Liber Diurnus Romanorum Pontificum, Lib. II, Titulum VII): "Disciplinam et ritum Ecclesiae, sicut inveni, et a Sanctis praecessoribus meis traditum reperi, inlibatum custodire; [second column]: "Disciplinam et ritum, sicut invenimus a Sanctis praedecessoribus meis canonice traditum, quamdiu vita in istis comes fuerit, illibate custodire." See also Pope Innocent I in his letter to Bishop Gubbio (PL 20: 552) regarding guarding or holding the traditions held by all.

[21] Gerhard Eger published (as found on 4/19/23 in https://sicutincensum.wordpress.com/2021/07/31/i-shall-keep-inviolate-the-discipline-and-ritual-of-the-church-the-early-mediaeval-papal-oath/) the following observations: Any such discussions must take into account the *Indiculum Pontificis* ("The Pontiff's Attestation"), an oath that popes seem to have sworn between the 7th and 11th centuries. In it, the pontiff-elect

as the insertion of St. Joseph in the Canon raised eyebrows, so to speak, of the knowledgeable theologians of the time. Hesitation for even such a relatively minor, or seemingly innocuous insertion, is based upon the principles of Apostolicity and longevity. If the liturgical texts and practices had been a certain way from the time of the Apostles or for such a long period of time (longevity), it was considered clearly the Will of God that the various elements of those liturgical texts were considered to manifest the Will of God, and therefore, inviolable. Popes did not consider themselves to have the authority to change ancient liturgical tests, and even if they did, piety and the virtue of religion would exclude even the consideration of changing them or departing from them.

To quote again Nicholas Gihr regarding the liturgical changes by Pius Vth:

---

solemnly vows to St. Peter that he shall preserve inviolate the doctrinal and liturgical tradition handed down to him by his predecessors and by the holy œcumenical councils and that he will act as a remora against the introduction of any novelties. This papal oath is preserved in the *Liber Diurnus Pontificum Romanum*, a collection of formulæ used by the pontifical chancellery which survives today in three MSS.: Vatican City, Archivio Segreto Vaticano, Misc. Arm. XI.19; Milan, Biblioteca Ambrosiana I.2 sup.; and the *Codex Claramontanus* now kept in the Abbey of Egmond-Binnen. A modern edition was published by the Jesuit Jean Garnier in 1680, reprinted in the *Patrologia Latina* (vol. 105, cols. 21-118). In 1869, Marie Louis Thomas Eugène de Rozière published an improved edition, followed by Theodor E. von Sickel's critical edition in 1889. Finally, in 1958 Hans Foerster published diplomatic editions of all three MSS. The *Indiculum Pontificis* appears as formula 83 in the Vatican MS., 59 in the Ambrosian, and 64 in the *Codex Claramontanus*. Sickel concluded that the texts of the *Liber Diurnus* developed over time and that the MSS that survive to-day represent its state during the reign of the Most Holy Lord Hadrian I, between the end of the 8th and the beginning of the 9th centuries. Some have argued, withal, that some of its formulæ date back as early as the pontificate of St. Gregory the Great. Gottfried Buschbell argued in 1896 that it stopped being used after 787, in his 1948 book on the Photian schism Francis Dvornik makes an excellent case for its continued use in the 11th century, when Cardinal Deusdedit wrote a compilation of canon law and included the papal oath therein.

> Hence the many changes and additions of the text of the Canon, which were produced during the Middle Ages, have disappeared partly already wholly since the reform of St. Pius V, in 1570. Since the thirteenth century, the Canon is, therefore, through its origin, antiquity and use, venerable and inviolable and sacred. If ever a prayer of the Church came into existence under the special inspiration of the Holy Ghost, it is assuredly the prayer of the Canon.[22]

II. On the Venerability and Inviolability of Received Liturgical Texts

The qualities of the Canon should be addressed somewhat individually to provide us with a sense of why the popes in the past considered the substance of the ritual of the Mass (and the other sacraments) as "hands off." In the above quote, the Canon was venerable, inviolable and sacred; these three qualities proceed from the Canon's qualities of "origin, antiquity and use." It is precisely the longevity and Apostolicity of the Canon that make its origin, antiquity and use the essential criteria for its being considered sacrosanct. The origin is two-fold. The first is the Apostolicity of certain of the elements of the ritual. The second is the fact that saints, popes, the Fathers, and men of profound erudition were the source of some of the other elements. It was also considered, especially in the case of longevity (antiquity), that an element that was started early on by a saint, pope, etc., was likely under the guidance of the Holy Spirit, precisely because God provided the grace to subsequent popes to leave that element in the liturgy for centuries. God would move a pope to remove it had it been contrary to His Will. The "use" of it by the Church for centuries was a testimony to the fact that God was pleased with that element of the ritual.

A. Venerable

The word *venerable* comes from *venerate*, which is defined as

---

[22]Gihr, *Holy Sacrifice of the Mass*, p. 581.

"not to be violated; not liable, or allowed to suffer violence; to be kept secretly free from profanation, infraction, or assault. To regard with feelings of respect and reverence; to look upon as something exalted, hallowed, or sacred; to reference or revere."[23] When something is venerable, one renders respect to it, which essentially means, "to observe carefully." Respect implies that there is a certain decorum in relation to how a person or thing is treated, *i.e.*, we observe caution in relation to our own actions in regard to the person or thing in order to make sure no offense to the thing occurs, but also so that our actions reflect the good we recognize in the thing.

The ritual of the Mass, as it has come down to us from times past is venerable precisely because some of the elements come directly from God, *i.e.*, the Divine Positive Law and Natural Law, which of their own impose limits on how one's actions bear upon the ritual. Yet, the ancient ritual can be considered venerable by virtue of the fact that there was nothing in it that was contrary to the Divine Positive Law and Natural Law itself. Furthermore, the longevity was a reflection of the Will of God, as discussed above, and so one was very careful not to offend God by going contrary to His Will be removing elements of antiquity or longevity, or that were introduced by saints who knew the Mind of God. Hence, any attitude of subjecting the liturgy's forms to one's own desires, whims or the spirit of the age would have been consider impious and, on a certain level, sacrilegious. It was a holy thing, a sacred thing.

Thc ancient liturgy is an expression of the doctrines of the faith to which the pope must assent and ought to cherish. Hence, even if there is perceived the need to make changes to the liturgy, great circumspection and caution was practiced in order to avoid any semblance of altering the faith, but also to revere the very expressions of the faith in the liturgy. The fact that the liturgy embodied the holy faith was itself a reason for its venerableness. It is for this reason that a pope must have a desire for the religious integrity to be preserved in

---

[23] *Oxford English Dictionary*, p. 3603.

the liturgy, and this would come in the form of a recognition that the ancient rites already contained that religious integrity. In fact, in the ancient Missal is a Postcommunion petitioning God to give the Church that very religious integrity.[24]

At the root of all of this was the virtue of basic piety in which one revered one's ancestors and parents along with basic Fear of the Lord, in which one offers reverence to God (and to sacred things). The fear in Fear of the Lord is not fear of God, but fear of our ability as sinners, as well as people suffering from darkness of the intellect due to original and actual sin, to offend God by what we do. The pope would avoid all liturgical changes *ad experimentum*, since such "experiments" could run the risk of offending God. Supernatural prudence and following the principles laid out over the course of the tradition would result in decisions being made regarding liturgical changes that were cautious and true to the tradition, when they needed to be made. Supernatural prudence would also result in a true grasp of circumstances, and hence, the Church was slow to make changes precisely during a time when major revisions would be being called for due to the spirit of an age. There was great safety in sticking to the ancient rites as a way of avoiding offending God unknowingly.

B. Inviolable

Given all of this, one can see why the popes, saints and theologians throughout time considered the ancient rites as inviolable, at least in certain elements which had the quality of Apostolicity and longevity. Inviolable is defined as "not to be violated; not liable or allowed to suffer violence; to be kept secretly free from profanation,

---

[24]See *Missale Romanum* (1962) Postcommunion for *Commune Unius aut Plurium Summorum Pontificum*: "Refectione sancta enutritam guberna, quaesumus, Domine, tuam placatus Ecclesiam: ut potenti moderatione directa, et incrementa libertatis accipiat et in religionis integritate persistat" ("Govern by holy refreshment with Thy nourishment to the appeasement of th Church, we ask, O Lord, that directed by powerful guidance [the Church] may receive an increase in liberty and persist in the integrity of religion.")

infraction, or assault."[25] Violence is action contrary to the nature of a thing, and so the ancient rituals were considered to be inviolable in their substance (nature). Popes in the past did not view themselves as having the right to modify them, even in the *accidentalia,* unless the criteria which we have discussed obtains, and even then with great caution and reticence. The fact that modern man seems prone to subject everything to his own judgment and choice of will would have been considered a serious moral and spiritual defect. It is precisely because the liturgy is considered inviolable that it went centuries without change and which is why when the popes suppressed rites; it is because the rites contained in them things that were not inviolable due to their lack of longevity (antiquity) and Apostolicity. Even the promulgation of "new rites" was one in which it was a codification of what was in fact venerable, inviolable and sacred because of their antiquity and source.

C. Sacred

All of this leads to the observation of Pope Benedict the XVI that "What earlier generations held as sacred, remains sacred and great for us too, and it cannot be all of a sudden entirely forbidden or even considered harmful." The definition of sacred is "Religious in nature, association, or use, of or pertaining to religion, its doctrines, history, etc., not secular, or profane, ...by association with the divine."[26] Something is sacred because it possesses a quality that relates to God, religion or something divine. For example, a blessed item is rendered sacred by virtue of the fact that it now possesses a quality, or more specifically a relation to God, insofar as it becomes a means through which people can obtain grace, which makes us more like God. The ancient rituals were considered sacred because (1) of their origin, *i.e.*, Christ, the Apostles, the Saints or popes; (2) their content, *i.e.*, the

---

[25]*Oxford English Dictionary*, p. 1479.

[26]Deferrari, *A Lexicon of Saint Thomas Aquinas*, p. 981.

articles of the faith, the Divine Positive Law and teachings of the Church; (3) their longevity insofar as God's Will is expressed by His regulation of history and the elements of the liturgy due to His desire for exactitude in worship of Him; (4) and the fact that thousands of saints, popes, bishops and priests had offered the rites in its substance throughout time. Even a minimal amount of humility left one recognizing one's unworthiness to change any parts of the ancient rituals, save by the command of the pope alone and even then with a certain "fear and trepidation." Humility itself kept popes reticent to make changes, and even then with great Fear of the Lord and caution.

Conclusion

If one takes into consideration all that has been covered in this text, one cannot but conclude that even if the pope has rights of determination due to his authority in relation to various elements of the liturgy, the exercise of the right was only done for either the most serious of reasons or to add saints to the calendar, update a feast based on a papal definition, and things of this sort. The very concept that modern man was different, and therefore, wide sweeping changes were necessary in the liturgy would have been considered a sign of a godless mentality.[27] The faithful must pray, as the traditional Postcommunion the Mass of the common for the popes envisions, that the Church will maintain religious integrity within the rites of the Mass and sacraments. Such a faithfulness on the side of the pope is only possible through grace.

---

[27]Even the changes to the ancient rite of Mass considered by Bugnini, Pius XII and *Sacrosanctum Concilium* 150 years prior would have been considered a violation of the very sacrosanct liturgy.

Conclusion

There are two extremes when considering the authority of the papacy over the liturgy. Historically, the Protestants held that the pope had no authority, despite their exercising authority over the liturgy in making determinations as to how future Protestants would worship. We also see this among some today who assert that the pope has no authority to make liturgical determinations. Regardless of the fact that this is contrary to the teachings of the saints, popes, and the Council of Trent, it is against historical fact. That the members of the Church had accepted liturgical changes in the past was a sign of the *sensus fidelium, i.e.,* that the pope does have the authority to suppress rites, to change them, etc. However, even the Church herself puts restrictions on that authority by virtue of the fact that the Council of Trent said the pope had the authority over the liturgy, save the substance of the sacraments. So not even the Church considers the papal authority over the liturgy to be absolute. This leaves the discussion in a place where the real issue is not whether the pope has authority over the liturgy, but what kind, to what extent, in what manner and with what restrictions. We will not recount those here, but hopefully the two extremes can be avoided in relation to the extent of papal authority.

Further discussion and research is needed on the pope's obligation to protect the sacraments and the sacred rites. Despite the fact that he has rights of determination over certain aspects of the rites, he also has the obligation to exercise his authority to protect the sacred rites from heretics changing them, error creeping in, unsound liturgical practice occurring, elements contrary to the tradition, etc. His authority is not just one of determination, but one in which he enforces in the members of the Church a faithfulness to those things over which he has the authority to preserve. Since he is the Vicar of Christ, the visible head of the Church on earth, it is his obligation to make sure the Will of God is implemented in the liturgy by observing the long-standing practices.

Any reading of this text will reveal that this is just a beginning.

Any discussion about the nature and limits of papal authority over the liturgy has to be based on Catholic principle and teaching as understood in the tradition. It was never the intention of the author to do an exhaustive study of the topic, but to simply provide a set of basic principles as a common reference upon which further discussion could be based. Obviously, this is done with full respect for the office of the papacy and willingness to follow the truth wherever it leads, regardless of the personal cost. We just have to do our part to make sure that the glory of God is maximized in the liturgy and that His Will is done in the sacred rites, regardless of our own desires and dispositions.

Bibliography

Acta Apostolicae Sedis: Commentarium Officiale. Typis Polyglottis Vaticanis. Roma. 1909.

Attwater, Donald. *A Catholic Dictionary.* The MacMillan Company. NewYork. 1941.

Ballerini, Antonius. *Compendium Theologiae Moralis*. Ex Typographia Polyglotta. Roma. 1878.

Michael Behe. *Darwin's Black Box*. Touchstone, New York. 1996.

Bellarminus, Robertus. *Opera Omnia.* Apud Ludovidicum Vives Editorem. Paris. 1870.

Bouix, D. *Tractatus de Jure Liturgico*. Apud Jacobum Lecoffre et Scoios. Paris. 1853.

Bouyer, Louis. *The Memoirs of Louis Bouyer: From Youth and Conversion to Vatican II, the Liturgical Reform, and After.* Angelico Press. Kettering, OH. 2015.

Bugnini, Annibale. *The Reform of the Liturgy: 1948-1975.* Trans. Matthew J. O'Connell. The Liturgical Press. Collegeville, MN. 1990.

Catechismus Catholicae Ecclesiae. Libreria Editrice Vaticana. 1997.

*The Catholic Encyclopedia.*The Gilmary Society. New York. 1929.

The Catholic Encyclopedia Dictionary. The Gilmary Society. New York. 1941.

Compact Edition of the Oxford English Dictionary. Complete Text: Reproducd Micrographically. Oxford University Press. 1971.

Crofts, A.M., *The Fullness of Sacrifice: Doctrinal and Devotional Synthesis on the Mass – Its Foretelling, Foreshadowing and Fulfilling.* The Newman Press. Wesminster, MD. 1953.

Daughters of St. Paul, *The Liturgy Selected and Arranged by the Benedictine Monks of Solesmes.* St. Paul Editions. Boston, MA. 1972.

Davies, Michael. *Cranmer's Godly Order: The Destruction of Catholicism Through Liturgical Change (Liturgical Revolution).* Angelus Press. St. Mary's, KS. 2015.

De Mattei, Roberto. *Saint Pius V: The Legendary Pope Who*

Excommunicated Queen Elizabeth I, Standardized the Mass, and Defeated the Ottoman Empire. Sophia Institute Press. Manchester, NH. 2021.

Deferrari, Roy, J., ed. *A Latin-English Dictionary of St. Thomas Aquinas.* St. Paul Editions. Boston. 1986.

---. *A Lexicon of Saint Thomas Aquinas*. Catholic University of America Press in collaboration with Preserving Christian Publications and reprinted by Loreto Publications. 1949 edition.

Denzinger, Henricus and Adulfus Schönmetzer. *Enchiridion Symbolorum: Definitionum et Declarationum de Rebus Fidei et Morum*. Herder. Friburg. 1976.

Edwards, Paul. *The Encyclopedia of Philosophy.* Macmillan Publishing Co. New York. 1972.

Fiedrowicz, Michael. *The Traditional Latin Mass: History, Form and Theology of the Classic Roman Rite.* Angelico Press. Brooklyn, NY. 2020.

Franzelin, Ioannis Bapt. *Tractatus de Sacamentis in Genere.* Editio Quinta. Ex Typographia Pontificia in Instituto Pii IX. Roma. 1910.

---. *Tractatus de divina traditione et scriptura.* Marrietti. Roma. 1870.

Jones, Kenneth C. *Index of Leading Catholic Indicators: The Church Since Vatican II.* Oriens Publishing Company. 2003.

Jurgens, William. *Faith of the Early Fathers: A Source-book of Theological and Historical Passages.* Liturgical Press. Collegeville, MN. 1979.

Gihr, Nicholas. *The Holy Sacrifice of the Mass: Dogmatically, Liturgically, and Ascetically Explained.* B. Herder Book Company. St. Louis, MO. 1949.

Lewis, Charlton and Charles Short. *A Latin Dictionary.* Clarendon Press. Oxford. 1975.

The Liturgy. Selected and Arranged by the Benedictine Monks of Solesmes. Translated by the Daughers of St. Paul. St. Paul Editions. 1962.

Knox, Ronald. *Enthusiasm: A Chapter in the History of Religion,*

with Special Reference to the XVII and XVIII Centuries. Oxford University Press. New York. 1950.
Kenrick, Franciscus Patricius. *Theologia Dogmatica quam Concinnavit.* Dessain. Mechlina. 1859.
Kwasniewski, Peter, ed. *From Benedict's Peace to Francis's War. Catholics Respond to the Motu Proprio Traditiones Custodes on the Latin Mass.* Angelico Press. 2021.
---. True Obedience. Complete
Lachman, Gary. *Turn off Your Mind : the Mystic Sixties and the Dark Side of the Age of Aquarius.* Consortium Book Sales and Distribution. New York. 2001.
Migne, J.P. *Patrologia Latina.* Paris. 1844.
Nevins, Albert J. *The Maryknoll Catholic Dictionary.* Dimension Books. Grosset & Dunlap. New York. 1964.
Oppenheim, Philippus. *Institutiones Systematico-Historicae in Sacram Liturgiam.* Domus Editorialis Marietti. Roma. 1820.
Ott, Ludwig. *Fundamentals of Catholic Dogma.* TAN Books and Publishers, Inc. Rockford, Il. 1974.
Pallen, Conde and John Wynne. *A New Catholic Dictionary.* The Universal Knowledge Foundation. New York. 1929.
Parente, Pietro, Antonio Piolanti and Salvatore Garofalo. *Dictionary of Dogmatic Theology.* The Bruce Publishing Company. Milwaukee. 1952.
Prummer, *Manuale Theologiae Moralis: Secundum Principia S. Thomae Aquinatis: in Usum Scholarum.* B. Herder. Friburgi Brisgoviae. 1931.
Reid, Alcuin. *The Organic Development of the Liturgy.* 2nd ed. Ignatius Press. 2005.
Ripperger, Chad. *Binding Force of Tradition.* Sensus Traditionis Press. Casper, WY. 2013.
---. *Consensus of the Fathers and Theologians.* Sensus Traditionis Press. Casper, WY. 2020.
---. *Dominion: The Nature of Diabolic Warfare.* Sensus Traditionis Press. Casper, WY. 2022.
---. *Magisterial Authority.* Sensus Traditionis Press. Casper, WY. 2014.

---. *Metaphysics of Evolution.* Books on Demand. Norderstedt, Germany. 2012.

---. *The Morality of the Exterior Act in the Writings of St. Thomas Aquinas. Warfare.* Sensus Traditionis Press. Casper, WY. 2018.

---. *The Nature and Psychology of Diabolic Influence.* Sensus Traditionis Press. Casper, WY. 2022.

---. *Topics on Tradition*. Sensus Traditionis Press. Casper, WY. 2013.

Schaff, Philip and Henry Wace, eds. *Nicene and Post Nicene Fathers.* Second Series. Peabody, MA. 2004.

Schroeder, Rev. H.J., O.P., trans., *Canons and Decrees of the Council of Trent*. B. Herder Book Co., St. Louis. 1930.

Spirago, Francis. *The Catechism Explained: An Exhaustive Exposition of the Catholic Religion.* Tan Books and Publishers. Rockford, IL. 1993.

Thomas Aquinas. *Thomae Aquinatis Opera Omnia*. Iussu Impensaque Leonis XIII, edita. Roma: ex Typographia Polyglotta et al. 1882.

Turcemata, Thomas. *Summa Ecclesiae*. Roman edition. 1560.

Vacant, A., E. Mangenot and E. Amann., E. *Dictionnaire de Théologie Catholique.* Librairie Letouzey et Ané. Paris. 1931.

Von Cochem, Martin. *The Incredible Catholic Mass: An Explanation of the Mass.* TAN Books and Publishers. Rockford, IL. 1997.

Webster's New World Dictionary. The World Publishing Company. New York. 1961.

Wuellner, Bernard J. *A Dictionary of Scholastic Philosophy.* 2nd ed. Bruce Publishing Company. Milwaukee. 1966.

---. *Summary of Scholastic Principles.* Loyola University Press. Chicago. 1956.

Made in the USA
Las Vegas, NV
21 November 2023

81295831R00132